WHAT REA
FA

"I wish my parents had read this book before I started having questions about Church history and doctrine. [It teaches] how to intelligently search for answers and to know what to do with them."

—Andrew S., age 24, Boise, Idaho

" . . . comes as an answer to my prayers for guidance in mentoring my children through the maze of questions and doubts that seem to bombard them at every turn. What a beautiful handbook for parents, teachers, and all who question!"

—Kimberly E., age 46, Rexburg, Idaho

"It's a great read—I was intrigued! I love the explanation about simplicity beyond complexity. I was able to relate [that to] experiences from my own life. I had never really thought about it [but] having this new point of view will be very helpful when I'm faced with unexpected, faith-challenging experiences."

—Scott S., age 33, Trumbull, Connecticut

" . . . deeply resounds with me. It is refreshing and joyfully honest and encouraging. Spiritual healing comes from feeling understood and validated, and I felt that way over and over while reading."

—Elizabeth C., age 20, Provo, Utah

"Going into my thirties, I felt like I was in a spiritual free fall. [Looking back now,] I understand that I was not falling, but that my spirit was maturing into a new level. This book helped to create within me a space free from conflict, full of hope, allowing God to reach me and speak peace to my mind."

—Paul S., age 48, Boise, Idaho

"This book made me realize that you don't need to fear that there is something out there that could destroy your faith. The tools are there, the divine help is there. We just need to educate ourselves how to understand and tap into that power. I understand better that 'faith casteth out fear'. That's why this book is so important."

—Elizabeth M., age 36, Preston, England

The book's core message "has had a profound influence on my life. It changed my perspective on the gospel life. With this newly discovered depth I [have] realized that I could take all experiences (good and bad) to deepen my discipleship, making me more receptive to [spiritual] promptings."

—Nathan L., age 26, Toronto, Canada

"Wow. A helpful framework to understand the role of uncertainty in developing faith. [Helped me realize] that inner conflict, doubt, seeming contradictions, even near hopelessness and fear, [can all be] building blocks to stronger, [more] fulfilling lives."

—Travis R., age 36, Fairfield, Connecticut

Faith Is Not Blind

BRUCE C. HAFEN
MARIE K. HAFEN

DESERET
BOOK

Salt Lake City, Utah

TO THE MEMORY OF B. WEST BELNAP

who taught us to see
that
faith is not blind

Image on p. 61, *The Disciples Peter and John Running to the Sepulchre on the Morning of the Resurrection*, Eugene Burnand/Bridgeman Images

Visit us at deseretbook.com

Library of Congress Cataloging-in-Publication Data
Names: Hafen, Bruce C., author. | Hafen, Marie K., author.
Title: Faith is not blind / Bruce C. Hafen, Marie K. Hafen.
Description: Salt Lake City, Utah : Deseret Book, [2018] | Includes bibliographical
   references.
Identifiers: LCCN 2018035175 | ISBN 9781629725185 (paperbound)
Subjects: LCSH: Faith. | Christian life—Mormon authors. | The Church of Jesus
   Christ of Latter-day Saints—Doctrines. | Mormon Church—Doctrines.
Classification: LCC BX8656 .H34155 2018 | DDC 248.4/89332—dc23
LC record available at https://lccn.loc.gov/2018035175

Printed in the United States of America
PubLitho, Draper, Utah

10 9 8 7 6 5 4 3 2

Contents

Contents

Acknowledgments

This book, like our lives, is a collaboration. But for purposes of clarity, Marie is the "I" in the Prologue and Epilogue, and Bruce is the "I" in the remaining chapters.

We are most grateful to Hal Boyd, Eric d'Evegnee, Holden d'Evegnee, Sarah d'Evegnee, Daniel Hafen, Tom Hafen, Martha Johnson, Kevin Knight, Lisa Roper, Bud Scruggs, John Tanner, Karen Tiffiletti, Emily Watts, and Jed Woodworth for their insights on earlier drafts.

PROLOGUE

"Listen Below the Noise"

The barren hills of the Judean Wilderness rolled out in every direction from where we stood overlooking Wadi Qelt, a river valley and ancient road between Jerusalem and Jericho. We wondered out loud to each other how a mortal could survive forty days of fasting in this country the way Christ had. Suddenly our thoughts were jolted by the sound of artillery fire in the distance. With a closer listen, we realized the noise was coming from a shooting range, and it was not near enough to do us harm. But the sound of the rapid fire ripped at our spiritual senses and abruptly changed the focus of the moment.

As we turned to go back to our car, a friend traveling with us asked if she could have just a few more minutes there. We watched her walk a bit farther down into the wadi and a few minutes later walk back up, while the caustic rattle of machine guns sounded only a few hills away. It wasn't until we were on the shores of the Sea of Galilee a day or two later that she shared what she had heard between the lines of gunfire. "I was so annoyed by how those guns were making it hard to feel the Spirit," she said. "But then I heard a thought come up from that dry soil as clearly as if someone had spoken it: 'Listen below the noise.' As I paid closer attention to what I was sensing, the thought grew into a full message: 'Listen below the noise. I made these hills. I am the Creator. All the gunfire is just superficial noise to me. I can blow it away in a breath. I put the pulse in this Earth. I put the same pulse in you. Listen below the noise for My voice . . . and stick with Me.'"

Metaphorically and literally speaking, our times are loaded with gunfire. The crossfire of these days seems constant and can keep us spinning in conflict, confusion, and conundrums brought on by loud and competing voices. We live in a complex world. The relentless chaos can make us feel like goldfish in a blender bowl with a three-year-old at the switch.

We can't, in offering you this book, stop the three-year-old or the gunfire, but we hope we can help you learn to listen below the noise—the noise in the world and the noise in you. We aren't attempting here to resolve all of the issues you may be confronting. But we are hoping you find in these pages a pattern for how to think about your questions and how, through grappling with them, to nourish your faith. We hope to help you make calm of the chaos. We hope to help you hear Him.

CHAPTER 1

Faith Is Not Blind.
Or Deaf. Or Dumb.

When I stood at the pulpit for my missionary farewell at age nineteen, even after much prayerful searching, I was stuck on the difference between knowing and believing. I couldn't honestly say, "I know the gospel is true." I knew some people expected me to say those words. But, in good conscience, I could only say, "I believe it's true." Noticing a nearby potted plant, I said my faith was like that plant—and I believed it would grow.

Then, toward the end of my experience in that era's one-week version of today's Missionary Training Center, we practiced giving our companions the first missionary discussion. As I taught about the Apostasy, a supervising returned missionary stopped to listen. He interrupted me to say, "Elder, bear your testimony there. Say you *know* the true Church must have twelve Apostles today, like Christ's original Church." I politely said that I would gladly testify to a real investigator, but in that practice setting, it was a little too personal for me to say "I know" on that point. He pushed back: "Twelve Apostles, Elder. I want to hear your testimony." Feeling a little stung, I said quietly, "I think Christ's Church today has fifteen Apostles, not twelve." He pulled up a chair and asked, "Do we have a little problem here, Elder?"

Then, thankfully, we were interrupted. But I was distressed that my level of belief—honest and deep as it was—might not be enough for a missionary. I thought back on all those nights before my farewell when I would use the building key I had been issued as an assistant stake organist and enter the St. George Tabernacle around eleven p.m. There I would play the tabernacle's fine pipe organ for an hour or so at full throttle, singing the songs of Zion all by myself, with only the tiny light on the organ console shining in that sacred old pioneer building. In my own way, I was bearing my testimony, but it was a little secret between the Lord and me, and it was still taking shape. I must have "known" *something*, but what?

Those memories returned when I read Richard Bushman's account of his sophomore year at Harvard, where his harsh encounters with irreligious skepticism left him feeling that he was "in hostile territory." Soon these pressures wore him down, until "religious agnosticism seemed like the only viable position given what we know for sure." He "did not know there was a God or that any of the things Mormons believe had actually happened." Nevertheless, he accepted a mission call. But "if I was such a doubter," he later asked in retrospect, "why did I go?"[1]

He has since "come to believe that in actuality my problem was not faith, but finding the words to express my faith." What he lacked was "language for Mormonism that made sense over the [Harvard] dinner table." He now thinks he actually "believed all along through that year—why else the mission?—but I was *dumb*, unable to speak."

Bushman has since spent a lifetime learning to communicate about religion "in a way that can be understood" by a secular audience rather than forcing them "to learn our language in order to understand us." What distinguishes his writing on Church history topics, then, is its tone, its language and vocabulary. Just as people unable to distinguish musical sounds are considered "tone deaf," many people in today's world have difficulty understanding religious language. So he consciously learned to write in a tone the secular audience could hear. *Faith is not deaf.*

At nineteen, like Bushman, I didn't have the words to express my faith adequately—except alone at the pipe organ. The distinctions among knowing, believing, doubting, and wondering are not trivial. But they are often unclear, because our experience is larger than our vocabulary. And when our once-untroubled faith abruptly confronts questions that leave us speechless, even temporarily, our faith can seem not only blind, but dumb. At that point we might want a book called *Faith for Dummies*—that is, when we feel speechless because of our spiritual growing pains, and we wonder if something is wrong. Would that mean we are also faithless? Probably not—but we might need a more complete vocabulary. A "growth in faith can [also] be thought of as an improvement in language."[2] *Faith is not dumb.*

So, as with Bushman's writing about Joseph Smith, my part of this book has turned out to be autobiographical. I've found myself trying to describe here my personal quest for a more "knowing" faith—the questions I encountered and the vocabulary I learned in seeking answers to them, a step at a time.

For instance, about "knowing," Elder Harold B. Lee of the Twelve bore a powerful witness of the Savior when he visited our mission. He quoted Doctrine and Covenants 46:13–14: "To some it is given by the Holy Ghost to know that Jesus Christ is the Son of God. . . . To others it is given to believe on their words." As I listened, suddenly I *knew* that he *knew*, and I believed on his words. That was only a step, but it was real. Belief or knowledge? Some of each. Later on, I gradually came to know for myself.

Just after my mission, a close friend asked what was the most important thing I had learned there. With the same honesty that had restrained my language at my farewell, I found myself saying that somehow I now actually knew that God was real, that He knew me, and that I had a personal relationship with Him—a reality that has grown and has anchored my soul ever since. I later heard someone call that acute and poignant sense of a relationship with God "the closeness." When I heard her words, I knew what she meant and why it raised her level of trust in Him.

As time went on, I found that "belief" and "doubt" are not the only alternatives. Nor is it enough to decide if one is a "Mormon conservative" or a "Mormon liberal," as discussed later in this book. Such polarizing dichotomies not only don't help us, they often interfere with genuine spiritual growth. They can also keep parents and children, or leaders and Church members, from listening to and understanding each other. Too often, young people and other members ask sincere but too-skeptical questions—while their parents and leaders give them sincere but too-rigid answers. That's what was happening in my brief exchange with that returned missionary. It would be far better if we could each get out of our "gap" and really communicate.

As I began my mission, "my problem was not faith, but finding the words to express my faith." With that memory in mind, our purpose here is to offer words, stories, and concepts that, we hope, describe a faith process that leads to confidence and trust in the Lord and His Church.

Our hearts go out to those whose faith becomes unsettled by information or people or experiences that seem to cast doubt on their previous beliefs. Encountering surprises and uncertainties is actually part of faith's natural growth process. We have been through many such surprises; our language just reflects our experience. Working through such opposition is the only way to develop authentic, well-tested spiritual maturity. That is why John Milton couldn't "prize a cloistered virtue"—a virtue that "never sees her adversary."[3] True faith is not blind, or deaf, or dumb. Rather, true faith *sees*, and overcomes, her adversary.

CHAPTER 2

The Simplicity Beyond Complexity

We first met as students in a BYU religion class called "Your Religious Problems." We both solved our biggest "religious problem" when our friendship from that class blossomed into our marriage. For each class, a student would pick a religious question, do research on it, then lead a discussion. We each wrote a short paper on how we would resolve the problem.

Some of the students looked at Church history issues or criticisms of Joseph Smith. Others looked at doctrinal questions, and some just wondered how to live the gospel better. It was a blessing to explore these questions together in an attitude of mutual trust. Our teacher, West Belnap, then BYU's Dean of Religion, often let us struggle. He wanted us to reach our own conclusions. Yet he knew just when and how to guide us with an occasional nudge. He was teaching us how to be good students of the gospel even as he helped us strengthen our faith in it. That class helped us see that "faith is not blind."

We both know what it means to encounter issues that require deeper digging in both thought and faith. Few of today's questions are new ones. What is new is the volume of raw dialogue around these issues as facilitated by the internet—a tool that, as we all know, can create both clarity and chaos.

Seeking a little order for the chaotic part, we'd like to share a model of thought that tries to encourage both clear thinking and faithful choosing. When held together, thought and faith can interact to help us keep our spiritual balance—and help us grow. Let's start by taking a look at the natural tension between the ideals of the gospel and the realities of life.

When we are young, we tend to think in terms of black or white—there is very little gray in our perspective. And many youth and young single adults have a childlike optimism and loyalty that make them wonderfully teachable. They typically trust their teachers, believe what they read, and respond eagerly to invitations for Church service. New adult converts often have similar attitudes. Their cheerful spirit and outlook make a refreshing contribution to their wards and branches.

As time goes on, however, our experience with real life often introduces a new dimension—a growing awareness of a gap between the real and the ideal, between what *is* and what *ought* to be. A piano teacher explaining how practice makes perfect shared this image about setting high goals and striving to reach them—which captures the relationship between the real and the ideal: "A distant star, / but not too far / to lure us out into the firmament. / And tho we ne'er may reach it, / we have tried / and in the trying / have learned, perchance / to make an orbit of our own."[4] We stand on the earthly surface of reality, stretching upward toward our lofty ideals. Let's call the distance between where we are and where we want to be "the gap."

We first see the gap when we realize that some things about ourselves or about other people are not what we thought they were. For example, even at a Church university that one might expect to be warm and homey, a brand-new student can feel lost and intimidated. Or maybe she brushes up against a faculty member whose attitudes about the Church are more liberal—or more conservative—than she expected.

And when we become acquainted at an adult level with those who have been our heroes, we might begin to see their human limitations. For instance, maybe one of our parents disappoints us in some way. Or we might see a Church leader forget an important meeting or lose his cool when he's feeling stressed. Perhaps we try hard to be obedient and we pray for needed help, but the answer just doesn't come in the ways the scriptures seem to promise. As a new missionary we might experience a jarring surprise when moving from the exhilarating idealism of the Missionary Training Center to the sometimes perplexing realities of daily life in the mission field. Maybe we suffer a surprise setback with our health, or we bump into an unexpected conflict with a close friend or family member. We might run across information we haven't heard before about Joseph Smith or Brigham Young. Or maybe we encounter something posted on the internet that raises religious questions we don't know how to answer.

Such experiences can produce an unsettling sense of uncertainty, and we might understandably yearn for simpler, easier times. We might find ourselves becoming a little skeptical, or we may begin to ask questions that haven't occurred to us before. Not everyone will encounter these things in the same way, but as we grow and increase in our awareness, most of us do run into some uncertainty and opposition.

The fundamental teachings of the restored gospel are potent, clear, and unambiguous. However, even the scriptures contain some ambiguity. Consider, for example, the story of Nephi, who was directed to slay Laban in order to obtain a critically important scriptural record. That situation is charged with uncertainty until we realize that God Himself, who gave Moses the commandment not to kill, was also the source of the instruction to Nephi.

Also, the Savior once said, "Do not your alms before men, to be seen of them" (Matthew 6:1). But He also said, "Let your light so shine before men, that they may see your good works" (Matthew 5:16). Another example—the Lord has said He can't look upon sin with the least degree of allowance (see D&C 1:31). Yet elsewhere He said, "Neither do I condemn thee: go, and sin no more" (John 8:11). Justice is indeed a divine law, but so is the law of mercy. At times these two concepts can seem inconsistent, until reconciled by the higher doctrine of the Savior's Atonement.

God has given us correct principles by which we may govern ourselves, but these very principles may at times seem to be in conflict. Choosing between two principled alternatives (two "goods") is more difficult than choosing when we see an obvious contrast between good and evil. But learning to make such choices is essential to our spiritual maturity.

Moreover, today's society is filled with increasing dissonance and conflict on a host of political, cultural, and social issues. People on the extreme sides of these questions seem very certain about the right answer. But some people would rather be certain than be right.

So life is full of ambiguity, and learning to manage the gap between the ideal and the real is one purpose of the mortal plan. By divine design, we all face "opposition in all things" (2 Nephi 2:11). As Lehi's dream teaches us, some parts of mortality are certain and clear, as symbolized by the iron rod that marks the path to eternal life, while other parts of mortality are unclear, as symbolized by the mists of darkness. But the distance between where we are on the path and where we want to be at the tree of life remains. This distance can be filled with misty clouds, and those holding to the rod can't always see clearly ahead of themselves.

Let's talk about how to deal with that uncertainty. We'd like to suggest a three-stage model that builds on a perspective offered by the distinguished American judge Oliver Wendell Holmes: *"I would not give a fig for the simplicity [on] this side of complexity. But I would give my life for the simplicity on the other side of complexity."*[5] Stage One of our model is the simplicity on this side of complexity, innocent and untested. Stage Two is complexity, the gap between the real and the ideal, where we struggle with conflicts and uncertainty. Stage Three is the simplicity beyond complexity, a settled and informed perspective that has been tempered and tested by time and experience.

For example, we recently attended a Latter-day Saint testimony meeting for some of the women inmates at the Utah State Prison—women separated from their families and from society by serious crimes and serious struggles. In bearing her testimony, one of the inmates said, "When I was a little girl, I often bore my testimony in church. In my innocent little singsong voice I would say, 'I love my mom and dad. I know the Church is true. My Heavenly Father loves me. Jesus suffered for my sins.' But today, behind these bars, I am saying those same words with new eyes and a new heart. Now I understand what the words really mean—I know the Church is true. My Heavenly Father loves me. Jesus suffered for my sins."

She was discovering the simplicity on the other side of complexity.

The challenge with those who remain fixed in innocent, idealistic simplicity is that their perspective may not yet have grappled with the realities of what Holmes calls "complexity." That's why he wouldn't give a fig for the untested idealism of naïve simplicity.

Some people still in the early simplicity of Stage One just don't see a gap. They somehow filter out any perception of the differences between the real and the ideal. For them, the gospel at its best is a firm handshake, a high five, and a smiley face. Their mission was the best, their ward is the best, and every new day will probably be the best day they ever had. These cheerful ones are optimistic and relaxed. They can weather many storms that seem formidable to those of a less sunny disposition.

Others in this stage may see the gap, but they choose—whether consciously or not—to ignore the terra firma of reality, thereby pretending that they have eliminated the gap, with all its frustrations. They cling to the ideal so single-mindedly that they just don't feel the discomfort that comes from facing the real facts about themselves, about others, or about the world around them. For them, perhaps the gap asks questions that are too raw, pushing them into a sense of denial that filters out painful realities.

When we don't see the gap or we focus only on the ideal while blocking out the real, our perspective lacks depth. If this is our paradigm, faith can be both blind and shallow, because it lacks awareness and careful thought. These limitations can keep us from extending our roots into the soil of real experience deeply enough to form the solid foundation needed to withstand the strong winds of adversity (see Alma 32:37–38). Growing deep roots requires that we learn to work through uncomfortable realities.

As we grow into Stage Two complexity, we can see reality despite its distance from our ideals—"things as they really are" (Jacob 4:13). Only when we see both the real and the ideal can we deal with the gap in a constructive way. If we don't grapple with the frustration that comes from facing bravely the uncertainties we encounter, we will lack the deep roots of spiritual maturity. If we don't see the problems that exist, we won't be able to help solve them.

However, despite the value of becoming aware of complexity, one's acceptance of the clouds of uncertainty can become so complete that the iron rod fades into the surrounding mists, and skepticism becomes not just a helpful tool but a guiding philosophy. A person viewing life only from the perspective of complexity will often eliminate his or her upward view of the ideal and focus exclusively on the real. In Stage One, the inexperienced person seems to have all of the answers, but may not yet know many of the questions. In Stage Two, that same person can have all of the questions, but few of the answers. In Stage One, faith is blind because it lacks awareness of reality. In Stage Two, faith is still blind if it sees complexity as the end of the journey of faith, because it has lost its vision of the ideal. A little learning, as valuable as that is, can be dangerous when left to think too highly of itself. The ability to acknowledge ambiguity, an important step in our spiritual development, is not a final form of enlightenment—it is only the beginning.

People who take too much delight in complexity's tools of skepticism sometimes try them out in a Church classroom or in conversations with others. They love to cross-examine the unsuspecting, just looking for somebody's idealistic bubble floating around so they can pop it with their shiny pin of skepticism. But when we burst those bubbles, we can lose harmony, trust, and the sense of safety that comes only when the Spirit is present. We need to look longer and harder at difficult questions and pat answers, but without lurching from extreme innocence to extreme skepticism. Today's world is full of hard-core skeptics who love to "enlighten" those who are stuck in idealistic simplicity, offering them the doubt and agnosticism of complexity as a seemingly brave new way of life.

I once learned how being overly realistic—getting stuck in skeptical complexity—can inhibit the workings of the Spirit. I had been on my mission in Germany about a year, long enough to learn that our work was hard and our successes few. I was assigned to train a new missionary, Elder Keeler. One day when I was away at a leadership meeting, he and another new elder met a pleasant woman at the door, but they didn't know enough German to talk with her. Yet he said he felt a strong spiritual impression that she would someday join the Church.

In fact, he was so excited about her that he forgot to write down her name—or her address. He knew only that her apartment was on some fifth floor in the middle of our huge, high-rise tracting area. He was sure he'd recognize her name next to the doorbell, so the next day we dashed up and down polished staircases for hours, but we couldn't find her. When I said we needed to go back to work, tears came to his eyes, and his lower lip began to tremble. He said, "But Elder Hafen, the Spirit really spoke to me about that woman." I muttered that maybe the Spirit was telling him to write down the name and address.

But to teach *him* a lesson, so I thought, I raced him up and down more staircases. Then, an hour or two later, we found her— Renate Wolfart. And forty years later, Marie and I were with Renate, her husband, Friedrich, and all four of their children and spouses in the Frankfurt Germany Temple. We watched through our tears as Friedrich, now a temple sealer, sealed their youngest daughter and her husband. That's a lesson I pray I won't forget: never lose sight of the "ideal."

The best response to the gap of uncertainty is to keep growing into Stage Three, where we don't just *see* the real and the ideal; we also *hold on* to each perspective—with eyes and hearts wide open. Looking through the lens of this simplicity beyond complexity, we can take action even when we wish we had more evidence before deciding what to do. For instance, we can sense the value of accepting a Church calling when we're feeling too busy to take on more duties. Or we can follow the First Presidency's counsel even when we don't understand the reasons behind that counsel—or when others around us criticize it. We're able to give the Lord and His Church the benefit of the doubt about our unanswered questions.

The choice to be believing at this stage is very different from mere blind obedience. It is, rather, a knowing and trusting kind of obedience. Instead of asking us to put aside the tools of an educated, critical mind, this attitude invites us to use those tools, coupling them with our confidence in the ideal, so we can improve the status quo, not just criticize it. Call it informed faith.

G. K. Chesterton once distinguished among "optimists," "pessimists," and "improvers," a comparison that roughly corresponds with Holmes's progression from early simplicity through complexity into mature simplicity. He concluded that both the optimists and the pessimists look too much at only one side of things. So neither the extreme optimist nor the extreme pessimist is of much help in *improving* the human condition, because people can't solve problems unless they are willing to acknowledge that problems exist while remaining loyal enough to do something about them.

Chesterton said the danger of the excessive optimist is that he will "defend the indefensible. He is the jingo of the universe; he will say, 'My cosmos, right or wrong.' He will be less inclined to the reform of things; more inclined to a sort of front-bench official answer to all attacks, soothing everyone with assurances. He will not wash the world, but whitewash the world."

On the other hand, he said, the danger of the pessimist is "not that he chastises gods and men, but that he does not love what he chastises." In being the so-called "candid friend," the pessimist is not really candid. "He is keeping something back—his own gloomy pleasure in saying unpleasant things. He has a secret desire to hurt, not merely to help. . . . He is using the ugly knowledge which was allowed him [in order] to strengthen the army, to discourage people from joining it."[6]

To illustrate the "improvers," Chesterton refers to the loyalty of women: "Some stupid people started the idea that because women obviously back up their own people through everything, therefore women are blind and do not see anything. They can hardly have known any women. The same women who are ready to defend their men through thick and thin . . . are almost morbidly lucid about the thinness of his excuses or the thickness of his head. . . . Love is not blind; that is the last thing that it is. Love is bound; and the more it is bound the less it is blind."[7]

An entry from the journal of my father, Orval Hafen, illustrates Chesteron's "improvers." He had moved beyond innocent idealism; his eyes were fully open to uncomfortable realities. Yet he had also moved past the complexity of being consumed with realism. Now his mature, more complete perspective gave him a new form of simplicity that permitted him to think and act productively, subordinating what he saw with his wide-open eyes to what he felt in his wide-open heart.

A friend of my parents was called as the bishop of their ward and said he couldn't do it unless my father would be his first counselor. Dad had earlier served in a stake presidency for ten years, and he was feeling very stretched with numerous obligations. So he wrote, "if it be possible, let this cup pass from me." He knew a bishopric's work could feel like "a continual grind [with] no let up." And "in some respects I am not humble and prayerful enough; I have not always been willing to submit unquestioningly to all the decisions of the Church."

But because he didn't feel he could "say no to any call that is made by the Church," he wrote, "not as I will, but as Thou wilt.'" He resolved to do his best, even knowing he might "chafe under the endless meetings." But "the work of the Church will have to come first. It will not be hard for me to pay my tithing and attend regularly, as I have been doing that." But "I will have to get to the temple more often" and "become better acquainted with the ward members and be genuinely interested in them," hoping "they might find it possible to feel the same toward me. Perhaps in my weak way I will have to try and live as close to the Lord as we expect the General Authorities to do." My father was an understated and honest man who still took his ideals seriously. His attitude makes me want to be as meek as my education has taught me to be tough-minded.

Holly's story gives us another example of someone progressing from innocent simplicity through complexity to settled simplicity. At age eighteen, Holly was extremely active in the Church, but in an "autopilot" kind of way. Then someone persuaded her that women ought to hold the priesthood. She was so convinced by this idea that she indignantly resigned her Church membership. A few years later, her college roommate was taking the missionary lessons. Holly decided to sit in. Her heart was touched, and she decided to pray for the first time in years.

As soon as she said the words "Heavenly Father," her frosted heart started to melt. She began to cry. In that moment she felt a tender connection with her Father in Heaven that, over the next days and weeks, led her to discover a relationship with Him that she hadn't known before. She called it "the closeness." Soon Holly was rebaptized. As she studied and prayed, her "closeness" to Him deepened. Stubbornness softened into trust. Then she said about her previous issues, "I trust Him. He knows what He's doing."

The prophet Alma knew all about these three stages: he taught that faith in God is a process, not an event, and that it requires great effort and patience. As recorded in Alma 32, he said that in the beginning, our simple desire to believe enough to exercise the first steps of faith does not yield a perfect knowledge—we actually "*cannot* know" with surety about the truth of Alma's words until we try the experiment and plant the seed in our hearts. As the seed grows, it expands our hearts and enlightens our minds until it is very real to us. But we're not done.

When we encounter the first surprises of complexity, we must tend the sprouting seed of faith with great care, so that when the sun burns hot, the sapling will not wither. By its very nature, faith can and will overcome opposition that is sometimes downright *withering*. Especially in the heat of those trials, we remember to look forward "with an eye of faith" to the time when we may partake freely of the fruit of the tree of life—the reward for our diligence and long-suffering.

And when we do reach the tree of life, there will be no more gap between the real and the ideal. We will have settled our complexities by a tough but trusting process of refinement through which, in pure and knowing simplicity, the real and the ideal become one.

CHAPTER 3

Simplicity, Complexity, and the Internet Age

The three-stage progression we've seen, from early simplicity to complexity, then to the mature simplicity beyond complexity, applies to many realms of personal growth. But for now, let's just apply it to dealing with questions about the Church in the internet age.

Here's a true story about a friend we'll call Mattias. After his mission and temple marriage, Mattias raised a family and, along the way, served in several Church leadership positions. Later we learned that Mattias ran into a series of doubts and questions through information on the internet that he said had undermined his religious faith.

When someone asked him what had happened, Mattias said that for years as a Church member and leader he'd been happily living in a kind of a bubble. Then some of his LDS friends came to him for answers to questions they had encountered on the internet. He said many of the issues were new to him—such as, how did Joseph Smith translate the Book of Mormon and the Book of Abraham, why were black Africans excluded from the priesthood until 1978, and did Joseph Smith really practice polygamy? Mattias's problem was not with what had happened in each instance, once he learned the details. Rather, he was distressed because he felt betrayed by not having previously known about these issues.

Because we knew and cared a great deal about Mattias, we wondered how these questions could have surprised him. Our experience had been so different from his. We had encountered such questions years ago as college students—not because we were digging into secret historical closets, but because we and our friends discussed these issues in an open atmosphere of faith as they came up. In the Church classrooms where we've sat ever since, these issues were not hidden, nor were discussions about them discouraged—although we recognize that this was perhaps not everyone's experience.

Remember when Mattias said that before these questions came to his attention, he had been living in a cozy bubble? That is an apt description of Stage One simplicity. Holly, so active in the Church that she was on autopilot, at first lived in the same bubble. Then the shock of bumping into Stage Two complexity felt to both Mattias and Holly like an earthquake that completely shifted the burden of proof in their minds about the Church. Almost without realizing what they were doing, they began to assume that the Church was simply wrong until it could prove itself right.

Holly's and Mattias's stories are instructive. They tell us that in this day of both the internet and the international Church, we need to do a better job of introducing our children, young people, new converts, and others to the process of learning how to deal productively with complexity.

During the recent decades of international growth, the Church has needed to simplify its curriculum, magazines, and other materials so that inexperienced Church members in many cultures can understand them. Because that approach can limit the availability of more advanced information, many people cheered in 1992 when the world-renowned Macmillan Company copublished with BYU the *Encyclopedia of Mormonism*. This four-volume work contains scores of careful, readable articles by qualified LDS authors on all the topics Mattias mentioned and many others. It has since been available on the internet and elsewhere. In addition, access to original Church documents has never been more open than in recent years, as witnessed by ongoing publications from the massive, Church-sponsored Joseph Smith Papers project that began in 2008.

The "gospel topics essays" more recently posted on lds.org are more visible than the *Encyclopedia of Mormonism*. They also reflect more recent research and provide extensive additional reference material. Hopefully these essays will help people notice some of what Mattias regrettably missed seeing. That increased visibility also sends a message about the value, in today's world, of having open minds and open hearts based on a prepared stance that is as wise as a serpent yet as harmless as a dove (see Matthew 10:16).

Such resources can help us work our way through complexity to mature simplicity. At that point, we are not just optimists and not just pessimists. We are open-minded believers who know that history and life are not always clear-cut and tidy, but we desire to keep learning and to improve the status quo, not just to criticize it.

Here are four suggestions that might help us move beyond the churn of complexity into the calm of tempered simplicity.

First suggestion: Faithful questions are valuable. Having a curious mind is a pathway to understanding and growth. However, there may be some who mistakenly assume that LDS culture disapproves of people who wonder. So when we have honest questions, some of us may feel unfaithful or even guilty. Is it wrong to wonder, or even to wander? We don't think so. The Church does not self-destruct under questioning and scrutiny. Rather, seeking answers and deeper understanding really can help us grow. As J.R.R. Tolkien said, "not all those who wander are lost."[8] So let us welcome questions and questioners.

Recall again Mattias's comment about living in a bubble. If he was, it wasn't because the Church consciously imposed that mind-set to keep him in the dark. His bubble might have been nothing more complicated than the innocent perspective of Stage One, not realizing that life has more colors than black and white. Good questions help us move on to the more realistic realm of Stage Two complexity, where we can see life in living color, with rich meanings that we must sometimes search to discover.

As we enter Stage Two, however, it's good to remember that becoming a doubting Thomas is not the end goal of discipleship. Being realistic is better than not seeing reality, but as we've seen, a myopic preoccupation with complexity can easily become a rigid pessimism that also blocks the search for truth. As one friend said, we don't want to be so closed-minded that we look at the world through a soda straw; but we also don't want to be so open-minded that our brains fall out. When we then choose to grow into the more complete and more faithful perspective of Stage Three, we won't let the issues we don't yet understand get in the way of the fundamental truths we do understand.

Second suggestion: Be cautious about the internet's weaknesses. One of the internet's great blessings, which is also one of its curses, is that it gives everyone—regardless of age or qualifications— unfiltered access to unlimited information. All of that unfiltered data, regardless of how reliable it actually is, can seem to have equal credibility. This lets the bloggers at the extreme ends of any spectrum seem as qualified to speak as if they were established experts. You can see their names right there on Google, just like the real rocket scientists—or sometimes instead of the real rocket scientists.

This unfiltered access offers great advantages, but it also invites grave dangers. It may take real effort to check the accuracy and motives of a website's authors, and we seldom have an experienced teacher nearby to answer our questions. The lack of responsible, effective filters makes the internet highly vulnerable to misinformation and manipulation.

When one friend was struggling with something he found online, we asked if he had also read the work of reliable LDS scholars on trustworthy sites. He said, "I can't trust those people—they're already biased in favor of the Church." We replied, "Don't you think the sponsors of negative websites have a bias *against* the Church?" Virtually everything online reflects *somebody's* bias—and those biases will not necessarily be self-evident.

Another risk of unfiltered access is that readers can't know which critical claims have already been discredited, and the negative sites' sponsors aren't likely to tell them. Actually, careful research by LDS scholars has responded thoroughly to the main criticisms about Joseph Smith, Brigham Young, the Book of Mormon, and other issues. It would be highly ironic if the internet were producing more casualties from critics now, when the Church's scholarly credibility has never been higher.

And speaking of biases, some feelings of doubt and inability to feel the Spirit are caused not by intellectual problems but by behavioral ones. That explains the request of one father when his son left home for college while still unsettled about his testimony. "As you continue your search for faith," he said, "please keep the commandments. Otherwise you will bias your search. If the affections of your heart are attached to the vices of this world, your head won't make you—perhaps won't even let you—believe in the virtues of God's world."

Third suggestion: Focus on the hugely positive doctrinal content of the Restoration, rather than becoming sidetracked with the details of how Joseph received that content. That big-picture perspective is central to the simplicity beyond complexity.

If we assume that Joseph Smith "translated" scriptures the way a scholar would, we misunderstand his role as a seer. He never said exactly how he translated, but it was clearly a process of revelation. "It was principally divine inspiration rather than [Joseph's] knowledge of languages that produced the English text of the Book of Abraham. His precise methodology remains unknown."[9] That is also true of the Book of Mormon—translated simply "by the gift and power of God" (Book of Mormon title page). But Joseph also told us: "Could you gaze into heaven five minutes, you would know more than you would by reading all that ever was written on the subject."[10]

As Richard Bushman wrote, "Unlike the scholarly translators, [Joseph] went back beyond the existing texts to the minds of the prophets, and through them to the mind of God."[11] Joseph apparently had access to the original sources from which all other scripture had come, a window into the entire heavenly realm—perhaps the same window through which Moses, Nephi, and John the Revelator saw. The pure and profound doctrines he found there revolutionized Christianity, restoring a true understanding of the nature of God and our relationship with Him; the nature of man—past, present, and future; the Fall, Christ's Atonement, the scriptures, and the very purpose of life. This astounding religious bedrock rings with such clear truth that it speaks for itself—with so much clarity that the details of how the Lord gave it to Joseph, even if we could understand those details, are less important than the content he received.

Fourth suggestion: Cultivate an attitude of meekness. When our idealism has been rattled by abrupt confrontations with realism, our attitude about what has happened is more important than what has happened. Elder Neal A. Maxwell said that *doubting* "can either soften or harden hearts, depending on [our] supply of meekness."[12] Meekness, a softness of heart and openness of mind, keeps the seed of faith alive. When we let adversity harden us, we choke the seed. But if we meekly retain our desire to believe—the attitude that first activated our experiment with the word—our believing heart lets the seed thrive.

So when we are jolted by hard experiences, we have a choice. We can either close ourselves to God in bitterness or open ourselves to Him in contrition. By choosing to have a contrite spirit, we bring our whole souls to God and give Him something to work with. Without that meek humility, the Lord will "not open unto" us, and "that happiness which is prepared for the saints" will be "hid from [us] forever" (2 Nephi 9:42–43).

Here's what that meekness looks like, illustrated in another missionary story from Germany. My companion and I were teaching a bright young American couple named Paul and Wendy Knaupp. They had read and believed the Book of Mormon and were eagerly preparing for baptism. Then Paul's family wrote him a letter warning him that Mormons were racist because they didn't grant their lay priesthood to black African men. Their family was sensitive to that issue because Paul's sister was married to a fine Christian man from Nigeria. Paul and Wendy felt hurt and betrayed. Why hadn't someone told them about this? Didn't we know that God treats all people equally? Yet they were bewildered, because they had felt sure that Joseph Smith was a prophet.

After venting their frustrations, they looked at me, the senior companion. I was speechless. This was 1962. I had never heard a serious discussion about race and the priesthood, let alone an explanation. But, suddenly recalling a fragment from my recent personal scripture study, I blurted out, "Let's read the story of Peter and Cornelius in Acts, chapter 10." Here we read that after centuries of restricting the gospel exclusively to the house of Israel, the Lord revealed to Peter that it was time to share the Savior's message with the Gentile world.

This event was a huge watershed in the history of Christianity.

Knowing of such a major change in ancient "Church policy" made it reasonable to think that someday He would open that door even more fully. That's what He did in 1978, when He revealed to President Spencer W. Kimball that it was time to extend priesthood and temple blessings to all worthy men as part of establishing the Church across the entire globe, for the first time in history.

Paul and Wendy called several days later to say they had prayed earnestly and wanted us to come back. Soon they were baptized, and in the years that followed they raised their family of five children in the gospel. Many years later we and the Knaupps were sharing memories about that pivotal night. I said the experience had taught me unforgettably that the Lord tells His missionaries what to say "in the very moment" (D&C 100:6). Wendy's main recollection was that somehow after our visit, the gloom they had been feeling gradually left them, and the light returned. Like Nephi, Paul and Wendy had sensed that God "loveth his children," even if they didn't "know the meaning of all things" (1 Nephi 11:17). They were meek and spiritually alive enough to know that the Lord loved them, so they trusted Him. They wouldn't let the things they didn't yet understand get in the way of all that they did understand.

The simplicity on the front side of complexity asks very little of us. But the simplicity on the far side of complexity asks everything of us, and we may need to bear that cost in multiple ways. For instance, we don't always move smoothly and quickly through complexity to "other-side" simplicity. Too many get stuck in the complexity. And because complexity is more nuanced and realistic than innocent simplicity, some bright people may think that mere complexity is better informed, more honest and authentic. Others may think that complexity is all there is, or that they can't get out. Others are so perplexed by it that they flee back to the remembered safety of early simplicity—even if they keep running into the unrealistic illusions they find there. But remember what Holmes said: "I would give my life for the simplicity on the other side of complexity."

The Knaupps discovered Stage Three simplicity by being open to a merely plausible explanation when it wasn't possible to know more. They didn't have a complete answer, but they sensed enough to lay their complexity at the Lord's feet. Their prayerful meekness allowed them to give Him the benefit of their doubt.

Our friend Holly found that same simplicity after she left the Church, then found it again with fresh, more open eyes. She had come to know complexity, with its conflicts and demands, but now she was meek enough to sense that complexity alone is not enough. Complexity does provide the texture, the contrasts, and the oppositions that give context and meaning to our choices and experiences. In that context, she heard the Restoration's message with new ears. Then she tasted the simplicity beyond complexity when she spoke those simple yet holy words with a new voice: "Heavenly Father."

Discoveries like the Knaupps' and Holly's are not small ones. They are part of the cosmic pattern of Adam and Eve, who left the simplicity of Eden for the complexity that began with the forbidden fruit. Then they gradually discovered that because of their encounters with complexity, their eyes were opened, and if they would repent and call upon God, they could now grasp the joy of full simplicity. They would not then return to the innocent simplicity of Eden but would ascend developmentally toward mature celestial life.

Because of the Savior's Atonement, they could learn from their complexity without being overwhelmed by it. In this life they would have joy, and they would one day be with Him again. And then they would truly comprehend, for the first time, the grand simplicity of being with Him and with each other—a fulness of meaning they would never have found in the simple innocence of Eden. In the words of T. S. Eliot, "We shall not cease from exploration. / And the end of all our exploring / Will be to arrive where we started / And know the place for the first time."[13]

As we make our way through our complexities, if we don't press forward by learning to give the Lord and His Church the benefit of the doubt, it won't be long until we are unwilling to go down the road of faith and sacrifice at all—the only road that leads to the deep simplicity of wisdom and light.

Complexity is valuable, even essential. But those who get stuck there will never know the simple yet profound joy of the Saints. "For ye receive no witness until *after* the trial of your faith" (Ether 12:6; emphasis added). Our sometimes cloudy tunnels of uncertainty are there to teach us, not just to torment us. And there is light at the end of those tunnels: the Light and Life of the world.

CHAPTER 4

Some Internet Soft Spots

We can't overstate the miraculous blessings the digital revolution and the internet have brought into our collective lives on this planet. We are living through a historical change equal to the invention of printing, driving cars, and flying airplanes. Yet such colossal advances always bring previously unknown risks— even when, as now, the benefits far exceed the risks. Among the risks in this case is that the digital revolution reduces the reliability of information.

Historical Quibbles

Each summer we have "Grandma and Grandpa Camp" with age-based groups of our grandchildren. Near July 4 last year, we chose a patriotic theme, asking each of the fifteen campers to give a short report on a person or event from America's founding. When our ten-year-old philosopher Peter gave his report on Benjamin Franklin, he summarized Franklin's life, told a couple of stories, then concluded wryly, "But he didn't invent electricity like everybody thinks!" He then sat down with a little flourish, and we went on to the next report.

The next day I told Peter I really liked his report and just wondered what he meant about Ben Franklin not inventing electricity.

He replied knowingly, "Well, he didn't. So what they told me in elementary school was not true." Still puzzled, I asked, "Were you talking about the story of the kite and the lightning?" He said that was part of it. So I asked, "Where did you learn so much about Franklin?" Peter replied matter-of-factly, "On the internet."

So I searched Google entries for "Benjamin Franklin." I found that some historians dispute Franklin's kite story, arguing that if it had happened as he claimed, the lightning would have killed him. Others say he knew what he was doing, avoided that risk, and proved the electric nature of lightning. As for "inventing" electricity, a youth website asked, "Did Benjamin Franklin discover electricity?" and answered, "Maybe not!" Years before Franklin, two Englishmen studied the science behind static electricity and were the first to call it electricity. Franklin showed its negative and positive elements; then Edison invented the lightbulb.

I recount these details not because I need to know who "invented" electricity, but because I wonder what leads a normal ten-year-old who reads online historical accounts to conclude that "what they told me in elementary school was not true." Should he also go on to say, as some people do in such cases, "I was lied to"?

Meanwhile, back at Grandma and Grandpa Camp, twelve-year-old Emma gave her assigned report on Betsy Ross. "Well, we really aren't sure if Betsy Ross made the first flag," she began. "That was just something her grandson said a hundred years later. So I won't talk about her. Instead I'll just show pictures of different American flags that have been used."

Not having previously noticed such a skeptical bent in Emma, I later checked Wikipedia's entry about Betsy Ross. I learned that while she is still "widely credited" with making the first American flag, "there is no archival evidence or other recorded verbal tradition to substantiate this story," which first surfaced in her grandson's writings fifty years after her death. But the Betsy Ross Bridge in Philadelphia remains "named in her honor."[14]

In the absence of adequate "archival evidence" to substantiate the Betsy Ross story, did Emma's elementary school teachers, like Peter's, teach her something that wasn't true? And is Betsy therefore a "discredited" historical figure whose story we should no longer accept?

The probabilities are very high that what is "widely credited" about both Ben and Betsy is true enough that our elementary schools can safely keep teaching their well-established historical accounts at a level that is understandable and age-appropriate. But what is it about online "research" that can undermine the confidence of our schoolchildren that their teachers are telling them "the truth"? And, whatever it is, could this part of the internet's soft spots also make some Church members wonder if *their* teachers or leaders are telling them the truth? If so, the problem is not with the students, teachers, schools, or Church leaders. It's with our need to understand why the internet works as it does.

Before popular websites took charge of both our research and our reasoning, most educated people knew that scholars often quibble over nuanced issues in old events. They are trained to do that because of the social value of our being open to any new discoveries. But prior to the internet, the socially perceived burden of proof was always on those who challenged established, reasonably well-documented interpretations.

Yet today, somehow, as we found with Peter and Emma, running across any criticism or a complicated difference of historical opinion can seem to shift the burden of proof to the traditional source—as if merely raising an apparently legitimate question is enough to win a guilty conviction in the court of public opinion. But most of today's readers aren't prepared to understand the criteria for shifting the burden of proof, let alone to know how to evaluate the qualifications and motives of witnesses.

In addition, prior to the internet, a teacher or parent who wanted to teach kids about Ben or Betsy or Washington or Jefferson could go to a library and find a source that fit the reader's preparation. But if we use the web, which can't discriminate among its readers by age or otherwise, we end up with what one scholar called "The Disappearance of Childhood."[15]

Unfortunately, some people aren't mature enough to weigh conflicting evidence and evaluate its sources. But sites like Wikipedia understandably want to earn and keep the respect of their most sophisticated and critical readers. So they "let it all hang out," inviting everybody on the planet to send in their differing evidence, and inexperienced readers (and their families and society) just suffer the consequences. When our children or others learn more than they can possibly comprehend about some highly charged subject (like history, religion, or sex) from internet browsing, we must all deal with the personal and social implications.

Peter and Emma are normal, healthy kids who just wanted to know if Ben Franklin discovered something important about electricity and whether Betsy Ross made the first flag. And if an official-looking website says we're not sure, they might interpret that as—they didn't. So those children lost confidence in Ben, Betsy, and their schoolteachers—even though a well-informed reading of the stories provides more experienced people with high enough probability that we're not going to remove Betsy's name from that Philadelphia bridge or take Ben Franklin's portrait off the $100 bill.

"Mythbusters"-style research tends to show that the popular versions of nearly all major founding stories (political, religious, or otherwise) contain inaccuracies or overstatements, or they leave out details, nuances, and unsettled questions. As LDS Church

Historian Leonard Arrington once quipped about the stories of hardship in settling the Western American deserts, "The remembered desolation of the Great Basin before the arrival of the Mormons became more formidable with each subsequent telling."[16]

Yet even after the mythbusters do their research, the bottom line of both the myth and its criticism typically remains. The criticism may clarify some detail, or prove that the folklore version is exaggerated, or show that some part of the evidence could use more credible sources. But the essential core of a well-established founding story that's been around and celebrated (and attacked) for a long time is usually still true.

Our point here is that well-known stories about people or events like Ben and Betsy have usually been told with Stage One simplicity—innocent, uncomplicated, widely believed. And the apparently authoritative criticisms of those stories represent Stage Two—casting doubt on the Stage One assumptions. Such criticism can propel readers from simplicity to complexity so fast that they no longer believe what they once did. This reality can make internet research an invitation to confusion.

For example, a friend who is a young single adult ward bishop often hears from ward members who have been rattled by a phrase or story that was taken out of its context in some event or statement in Church history. And they lack the experience to sense the need for more context; or they don't know how to find the context; or, despite feeling shattered, they still sometimes don't care enough to look for it. Their problem is not that they know too much about Church history, but that they don't know nearly enough. And they have been conditioned by the oversimplifications of social media to expect a short answer to any question. They often aren't interested in a long answer to anything—even if the true, complete story is very complex.

This makes it easy for Church critics, or someone unknowingly quoting a critic, to present some negative inference as a fact when it is not at all settled in the reliable research. The inference can appear deceptively negative when, as is often the case, some part of its claim is based on a true historical sliver—which makes the overall context crucial. But when listeners hear only the negative half-truth, they sometimes shift the burden of proof, so that (perhaps egged on by critics who don't disclose their motives) they put the Church on the defensive and in the wrong, until the Church can explain the more nuanced reality—and they may not keep listening to take in the nuanced explanation. This tendency, like the evidence questions about Ben and Betsy, easily allows people with a dark motive to discredit those they want to discredit.

Fake News

The current problem that bothers U.S. columnist David Ignatius most is that "people don't seem to know what's true anymore" about everything from climate change and "allegations about people we like [or] don't like" to the "political polarization" now infecting "every area of our common life—including sports. . . . *We're learning that social media can be tools of deception as well as truth.*"[17]

For instance, a grandmother who had raised her grandson recently received an email from someone posing as a police officer, saying the grandson was in jail in Europe for DUI and needed bail money. Another of her grandsons said, "Grandma, who loved and had spent years investing in her grandson, was sent into despair— one email from a fraudster and she seemed ready to jettison all of her dearly held confidence in her grandson. Church members are sometimes driven to distrust by equally ill-motivated and anonymous sources on the web."[18]

Social media's deceptive power now shows up in many places.

We can no longer "trust the reviews [we] read online" about consumer product quality—a problem that is "an internet nightmare."[19] And tragic acts of large-scale violence, like mass shootings, often trigger false, politically motivated stories that claim who or what caused the violence, vrooming virally across social media sites so quickly that the true news accounts can get lost in a kind of public semiconsciousness. Recent examples include a tragic shooting in Las Vegas and another in a Texas Baptist church.[20] Perhaps the most flagrant recent fake news problem is the Russian government's apparently fraudulent use of our major social media platforms to influence the 2016 U.S. presidential election—and American society's general perception of itself.[21]

In the largest study of fake news to date, MIT data scientists in 2018 found that false stories are 70 percent more likely to be retweeted than true stories, perhaps because they are more "engaging or provocative."[22] This research feeds into "a raging global debate about the ability of Silicon Valley companies to influence society. [The] internet giants are under intensifying scrutiny over *the power of their products and their vulnerability to bias or manipulation*."[23] That combination of power and vulnerability is not just unsettling but dangerous. The internet really can be manipulated for religious or many other purposes.

Merchants of Doubt

Riley grew up in an LDS home. After his mission and temple marriage, some comments from non-LDS friends at work made him feel he had lived such a sheltered life that he really ought to make what he called "a more objective study" of the Church's history and beliefs. So he began reading whatever turned up in his online searches about Church issues. The more he read, the more unsettled he felt. It never crossed his mind that he might be reading "anti-Mormon literature," which he already knew was so clever and suspect that it wasn't reliable. He thought he was doing objective, unbiased research. Eventually he didn't believe anymore that Joseph Smith was a prophet. Later on, he lost confidence in the existence of God. As it turned out, Riley had unknowingly and naïvely experienced a full dose of the internet's soft spots.

Soon after hearing Riley's story, we visited with another family whose relative had recently left the Church because of his doubts. These friends said a group with an aggressive anti-Church agenda had taken their relative's story public and funded its wide publication with the intentional goal of undermining the faith of other Mormons. Merchants of doubt. After connecting some dots, we realized that this aggressive group was also the sponsor of the website where Riley did much of his "objective" research. Because he didn't know how biased his source was, he hadn't filtered it to protect his innermost spiritual sense.

Riley's story reminds us of how the tobacco industry in the 1990s developed a strategy cleverly designed to undermine the public's confidence in scientific findings about the health risks of smoking. Rather than trying to prove that the ever-stronger science findings were wrong, the industry simply launched a campaign to cast doubt—any doubt—on those findings. Why just doubt? They knew they couldn't win an all-out argument about health risks, so they simply raised enough doubt to create indecisiveness and inaction among both the public and government regulators—and for several years they succeeded.

The tobacco industry's strategy exploited an important characteristic about the very nature of science—also a characteristic of history, which deals with events so old that we can't answer every conceivable question about them. Science writer Christie Aschwanden says science can increase or decrease our confidence in some propositions, but it can't produce "absolute certainty." Instead, "it's a process of uncertainty reduction."[24]

So the tobacco industry's "brilliant tactic was to turn this baked-in uncertainty against the scientific enterprise itself. While insisting that they merely wanted to ensure that public policy was based on" what the industry called "'sound science,'" the tobacco companies defined sound science in such a way that "no science could ever be sound enough. The only sound science was [absolutely] certain science, which is an impossible standard to achieve." As one prominent tobacco company employee wrote, "*doubt is our product,*" because it "is the best means of . . . establishing a controversy," thereby "undermining inconvenient science."

These "merchants of doubt" weren't really pushing for better knowledge. Instead, they worked to "amplify uncertainty, create doubt and undermine scientific discoveries that threaten their interests." For years that strategy worked so well for the tobacco industry that the same basic approach has since "served as a sort of playbook for [other] industry interests ever since."[25]

Today's religious "doubt merchants" exploit the same flaw the tobacco industry exploited. By raising any doubt that seems supported even by limited evidence, they make claims that, in effect, assert the Church is wrong until it can prove an airtight case—often under circumstances where it's impossible to prove anything with airtight certainty. This approach seems basic to "the anti-Mormon playbook. It explains why [critical] arguments that have been debunked still persist; it's because [in the internet age] the doubt they sow still works. The [critics] don't have to prove anything; they just have to make someone doubt, which is infinitely easier than producing conviction."[26]

But the doubt merchants can change the fair standard of proof only if we individually allow them to. Both common sense and our legal system tell us that someone accused of wrongdoing is presumed innocent until proven guilty. And whoever makes the accusation carries the burden of proof to confirm the guilt. Raising questions or doubts alone would never, legally or logically, carry that burden. One unresolved question can't offset a mountain of answers that *are* resolved. Perhaps we can't explain with certainty where one lost sheep is located, but that alone by inference doesn't mean the other ninety-and-nine are also lost.

Our encounters with doubts and questions aren't always imposed on us by a threat or an enemy. Whatever their source, they can be an opportunity to learn and grow from experience. We can do that so long as we leave the burden of proof in the same place where the Psalmist put it: "They that know thy name will put their trust in thee: for thou, Lord, hast not forsaken them that seek thee" (Psalm 9:10).

CHAPTER 5

Productive Ambiguity

Ambiguities, apparent contradictions, and paradoxes are all around us. Even true principles can compete with each other in confusing ways. Learning to accept those apparent conflicts long enough to work through them is an essential step in finding the simplicity that lies beyond complexity. Yet bumping into these conflicts can make us want to dodge the ambiguity so we don't have to deal with the tension it creates. Still, as Joseph Smith once said, "by proving contraries, truth is made manifest."[27]

This issue is relevant to our three-stage process. Many Stage One idealists who collide with Stage Two realism are so daunted by the "contraries"—contradictions and paradoxes—that they can't see how to keep moving into Stage Three mature simplicity. Some simply prefer reverting to the comfort of one viewpoint over carrying the discomfort required to navigate and, eventually, be enlightened by a continuing paradox—like justice and mercy. Yet to move from complexity to informed simplicity, we must remain open, learn to honor competing principles, accept the tension, and transcend an either-or mind-set. Then the tension becomes productive.

For example, during my time as Dean of the BYU Law School in 1987, Church President Ezra Taft Benson spoke "To the Mothers in Zion" in a Churchwide Sunday evening broadcast for parents.[28] He described motherhood as "the noblest calling of all;"

indeed, "motherhood has the greatest potential influence either for good or ill in human life."[29] After emphasizing the importance of having and nurturing children, President Benson said that through death, divorce, and other "unusual circumstances," mothers may be "required to work for a period of time." But he urged each father "to do all in his power to allow his wife to remain in the home caring for the children." And he expressed genuine empathy for childless and unmarried faithful women.

The morning after the talk, as my Family Law class began, Mitzi Collins, a student, raised her hand. "Dean Hafen," she asked, "could we discuss President Benson's talk from last night?" I nodded and suggested we talk right after class. Mitzi shook her head gently, "Could we talk about it right now? We really need to talk—now." I knew and respected Mitzi. She was the president of the Women Law Students Association, an excellent student, and a devoted Latter-day Saint. Then I saw virtually all of the women students nodding in agreement with her.

So we began a very open conversation about President Benson's talk that lasted until the class period ended. I learned from these students that already that morning some of the women had found notes left on their carrels by well-meaning but thoughtless male students who had written statements like, "Law school admission is so competitive. Please let a man have your place in our class." After class, I agreed to have a similar discussion with all of the women law students that afternoon in the student lounge.

When I later started for the lounge, I saw a crowd of students walking in another direction. I asked a student, "Where is everybody going?" He replied, "The Moot Court room. The Dean is going to tell us what the prophet meant!" Somehow my meeting with women students had become a meeting for all law students—to say "what the prophet meant"? I shuddered.

I don't recall everything I said, but I sensed—without then

having the conceptual framework to have put it this way—that I was witnessing a whole series of collisions between Stage One simplicity and Stage Two complexity. Many students were confused, and not many were looking for Stage Three.

Some male students, including those who had placed the notes on the women's carrels, felt vindicated by their narrow reading of some of President Benson's language. They were troubled by our growing number of women students, sometimes judging them as living out of harmony with Church teachings. They were also aware of what was then a burgeoning national movement to eliminate discrimination against women. For a number of them, some dimensions of the women's movement clashed with their idealistic view of gospel values—so now they were even more determined to remain unmoved in Stage One.

Others took the opposing view, tending generally to downplay what President Benson said if they didn't agree with it. They were stuck in Stage Two complexity. But Mitzi and many of her friends represented a third viewpoint, feeling caught in the gap between the ideal and the real. They had enrolled in our law school with idealistic visions of what they could do with their legal education, single or married. But now, because of the respect they felt for the President of the Church, they wondered if they had done something wrong. They sincerely wanted to follow the prophet. This law school had been their hope; now that hope felt dashed.

I first told the students that during my BYU–Idaho years, I had attended monthly Church Board of Education meetings with our senior Church leaders—including President Benson. I knew firsthand how they felt about the law school. I said, "The Brethren know you women students are here, and they are glad!" Both in public and in private, I had heard them express many positive variations on President Gordon B. Hinckley's oft-repeated counsel to LDS women: "Get all of the education that you possibly can. Life has become so complex and competitive. . . . You will be expected to put forth great effort and to use your best talents."[30]

At the same time, the general principles President Benson had taught about mothers later turned out to coincide with a key theme in the Church's "The Family: A Proclamation to the World," issued in 1995: "By divine design, fathers are to preside over their families in love and righteousness and are responsible to provide the necessities of life and protection for their families. Mothers are primarily responsible for the nurture of their children. In these sacred responsibilities, fathers and mothers are obligated to help one another as equal partners. Disability, death, or other circumstances may necessitate individual adaptation."[31]

I wanted them to know that these true principles applied to society as well as to the Church. Drawing on my own research in U.S. family law, I expressed personal concern that our society increasingly devalues motherhood—even though the social science research has shown for years that good mothering is critically important. I don't recall just what illustrations I shared then, but those data were similar to more recent research findings. A 2005 study, for example, found that 81 percent of American mothers considered their mothering the most important thing they do, even though only about half of all mothers felt valued in that role by society.[32]

Other data show that mothers are the best models to help growing children move through all the necessary stages of brain development. Thus, absent or ineffective mothering can stunt childhood brain growth, negatively affecting both families and society.[33] Stable marriages and stable parents—both mothers and fathers—are the key factors that determine children's well-being. And dysfunctional children contribute to an increasingly dysfunctional society.[34]

I added that our students' gospel perspectives equip them to understand marriage and parenting far better than most people do now. If our students of either gender were asked to tell other American law students what mattered most in their lives, their general priorities would probably sound much like President Benson's. That made it all the more important for the women in that group to gain a sound legal education and the analytical skills needed to help a society that is all confused about marriage and family life.

In summary, I said, almost nothing is more important than motherhood and fatherhood. At the same time, the Church encourages women to gain all the education they can, including, if they so choose, law school. And we all need prayerfully to apply these sometimes-competing principles to our own circumstances. The Brethren have confidence in our ability to do that.

The way many of our students had aligned themselves with only one of these principles illustrates today's tendency to live at just one end of a bipolar world. At times we judge other Church members too harshly, not allowing them the space to make personal judgments. Learning to understand and live with competing true principles is an essential skill—not only for law students, but for all the rest of us. That capacity is one of the hallmarks of settled simplicity in Stage Three. As we do that, we will learn for ourselves that "by proving contraries, truth is made manifest."[35]

As a second example, we can also feel the discomfort of ambiguity in our choices to make sacrifices for the Lord or the Church in the face of uncertainty about possible outcomes. That discomfort, sometimes even anxiety, actually tells us that our eyes are open to the implications and possible consequences of what we're doing—and why we're doing it. For instance, if I find a lost wallet filled with cash, it is perfectly normal—probably even desirable— for me to realize that I could keep the money rather than looking for the wallet's owner. That awareness makes my choice to look for the owner fully moral. I am then conscious of the choice to act, to risk, to extend myself—as opposed to an automatic, rote decision.

Often, probably too often, we speak of real sacrifice far too glibly, not acknowledging the ambiguity and anxiety we might honestly feel before bowing our heads in submission before God— especially when we can't possibly understand all the reasons why we must sometimes give so much when we know so little. As John Tanner said in describing the heroic sacrifices of pioneer-like family members, "In stories like these it is easy—too easy—to see the faith and miss the fear. But you can't miss the fear and trembling when it is your own history."[36]

The scriptures repeatedly illustrate this process—part of the core doctrine of walking by faith (see 1 Nephi 3:7). Think of the profound ambiguity in the moment when Abraham stood with a raised knife over his precious Isaac, knowing that the requested sacrifice contradicted everything that mattered to Abraham: the promises about his only son, his posterity, his promised land— everything, that is, except his unconditional love for the Lord.

Esther knew that her people were fasting and praying for her, but she also knew that she was risking her life by approaching the king. With fully informed faith, Esther said, "So will I go in unto the king, which is not according to the law: and *if I perish, I perish*" (Esther 4:13–16; emphasis added). The three young Israelites approached the fiery furnace in Babylon with the same conscious mind-set: "Our God . . . is able to deliver us . . . and he will deliver us . . . O king. *But if not*, . . . we will not serve thy gods" (Daniel 3:17–18; emphasis added).

Moroni faced the apparent contradiction of being tasked with writing a final witness on sacred plates, yet "because of the awkwardness of our hands" he felt unable to write with power, saying, "I fear lest the Gentiles shall mock at our words." Then the Lord taught him that if he would humble himself, He would turn the weakness to strength (see Ether 12:24–30). The Lord has a way of helping us resolve our ambiguities in ways that both stretch and strengthen us.

One young returned missionary left the Church because, he said, "the Church didn't meet my expectations." That viewpoint could simply reflect a modern consumer's view of decision making, but it can also trivialize his religion, perhaps because it doesn't get a high enough Yelp rating. Even so, it is likely that this same young man had experienced his own moment of Abrahamic ambiguity, when he needed to decide in whom, or in what, he most wanted to trust. Choosing apathy or choosing to trust the Lord and His Church could, either one, temporarily resolve one's ambiguity—even, temporarily, one's existential anxiety. But the long-term differences between the two paths are staggering.

If we can resolve our ambiguities with a believing attitude, our faithful choices will lead ultimately to our sanctification. Those whose faith is not blind "see with their eyes, and hear with their ears, and . . . understand with their heart." And that complete use of our faith senses will one day bring us to the feet of Him who said, "and I should heal them" (Matthew 13:15).

CHAPTER 6

The Head and Heart Paradox

There are some natural tensions between faith and reason, which offer an instructive variation on the theme of tensions between early simplicity and complexity. As we search for the right relationship between faith and reason, that process prepares us to reach for a yet higher form of resolution in yonder simplicity.

Just after my mission I enrolled in that "Religious Problems" class in which Marie and I met. As each of us chose a topic to study and share, many of the issues were similar to questions LDS young people wonder about today. For instance, one of our close friends from that class was the gifted and faithful Dillon Inouye. His question was, "Has the gospel of Jesus Christ really been restored?" Marie chose to discuss, "How can I bring the influence of the Holy Ghost more into my life?" My question was whether I should be a Mormon liberal or a Mormon conservative. I honestly wondered how much we should develop our own minds and think for ourselves, compared with how much should we rely on Church authority and spiritual guidance.

BYU history professor Richard Poll wrote an article during those years called "What the Church Means to People like Me." He said that most Church members fell into one of two distinct camps: they were either rigid, "iron-rod" Mormons, who unquestioningly wanted the Church or the Spirit to tell them exactly how to live, or "Liahona" Mormons, for whom the gospel pointed a desirable general direction but who tended to rely mostly on their own wits in deciding how to live.[37] Speaking of Poll's two categories, our friend Dillon said he would prefer to see an article called, "What the Church means to people like . . . God."

Dillon, Marie, and I and our classmates were experiencing what Catholic sociologist Thomas O'Dea had called "*Mormonism's most significant problem.*" In his 1957 book, *The Mormons*, he said the Church's "great emphasis on [higher] education" created a serious and unavoidable conflict for LDS college students, because the Church's literalistic and authoritarian approach to religion collided with the skepticism and independence fostered by university-level studies—just like the "ideal" confronting the "real." For O'Dea, that issue was a big one: "The encounter of Mormonism and modern secular learning is still taking place. *Upon [the outcome of this source of strain and conflict] will depend the future of Mormonism.*"[38]

Fifty years later, reliable research showed that—unlike with most other religious groups—the more education a Mormon has, the more likely he or she is to have a strong religious commitment. For example, some 84 percent of Mormon college graduates have high religious commitments, compared with 50 percent among Mormons who have only a high school education.[39]

I could see from BYU's growing academic stature how committed the Church was to higher education. And I had returned from my mission with enlarged perspectives that fueled my hunger, even my passion, for learning. I was close to some LDS university teachers whose examples motivated me toward learning. One of them told me that J. Golden Kimball said we can't expect the Holy Ghost to do our thinking for us. Another favorite teacher had a great love for literature and the arts, and he emphasized that students needed mostly their own discipline and personal creativity to develop their God-given gifts.

My piano teacher from my high school years was Reid Nibley, Hugh Nibley's younger brother. Reid was a spiritually reflective but professionally consummate artist. He taught me that higher sensitivity to music would increase my spiritual sensitivity, adding that the Lord had given us nature and the arts "to gladden the heart . . . and to enliven the soul" (D&C 59:18–19).

Then I encountered mentors who proceeded from different assumptions. My mission president, whom I loved and admired, introduced me to doctrines about knowing the Lord and relying on the Spirit. I came to prize those doctrines when I saw their fruits in missionary work. He often said, "Trust in the Lord with all thine heart; and lean not unto thine own understanding" (Proverbs 3:5). He emphasized Christ's total reliance on the Father: "The Father that dwelleth in me, he doeth the works" (John 14:10). So, to him, "Christ was the most un-original man who ever lived." He also warned against people who took literature and the arts too seriously.

I also grew close to a respected seminary teacher. When he asked what I planned to study at BYU, I said I wanted to learn all about history, literature, and philosophy. He replied with great concern that I should avoid those subjects because they can easily lead people into what he called "intellectual apostasy."

So my "religious problem" reflected the confusion I felt in trying to reconcile the conflicting viewpoints among these mentors. Our professor, West Belnap, said to me after my class presentation, "Well, some of our people have it in their heads, and others have it in their hearts. I think it's best to have it in both places." I understood that as a call for simple balance. That attitude helped me decide to reject an either-or approach to my question. I also began to see the problems with each extreme.

For example, I witnessed the conservative extreme of over-zealous religiosity. I was called as a stake missionary companion to someone who was sure the Holy Ghost was whispering to him almost constantly, down to the details of his thoughts and decisions. He carried a little book in which he often wrote long sentences to capture what he believed the Spirit was telling him. He would dust off his feet after we left the door of someone who wasn't interested in our message. Some years later, he concluded that the Church was misguided and that God had called him to reform the Restoration. He attracted a small but zealous following. Eventually his tendency to "look beyond the mark" ended in multiple tragedies for him, his family, and his followers.

I was later called as a counselor to two very different student-ward bishops who illustrated the broad spectrum of personalities and attitudes we find among Church leaders. One of them was highly authoritarian, rigid, and distrustful toward the academic disciplines. The other one was at the other end of the spectrum—free-thinking, critical, and academic. He was close to some General Authorities and liked to tell us about the strong differences of opinion among the Brethren. Then he began to see not just differences in viewpoint but serious personal flaws in these leaders. These concerns ate away at him, compromising his willingness to follow counsel from general Church leaders whose views differed from his own. Some years later he also bitterly left both the Church and his family.

These experiences reinforced my inclination to seek what I would simply call a balanced approach. I didn't need to make a permanent choice between my heart and my head. I could see that the tension between faith and reason has a very long history. During the time of Christ, He taught His gospel almost exclusively to people with a Hebrew background. Not many years after His death, Gentiles from the Roman Empire who had a Greek heritage began entering the Christian Church, until Christianity became the official religion of the Roman Empire in the fourth century.

That huge historical shift merged the Hebrew and Greco-Roman cultures, combining two very different religious traditions.

One historian said this merger superimposed the "entire Hebraic Tradition upon classical [Greek and Roman] culture."[40] And because Greek thought heavily influenced the Roman Empire, another wrote, "Here were two races [the Greeks and the Hebrews], living not very far apart [yet] in complete ignorance of each other. It was the fusion of what was most characteristic in these two cultures—the religious earnestness of the Hebrews with the reason and humanity of the Greeks—which was to form the basis of later European culture."[41]

Speaking of this historic watershed, BYU's Daniel Peterson wrote that the shift of Christianity's center of gravity from Jerusalem to Athens and the Greek-speaking world gradually cut the New Testament's ties to its roots in the Hebraic world of the Old Testament. The resulting Greek influence preserved Christ's words in the New Testament only in the Greek language. "Mormons," he wrote, "recognize in this [Greek absorption of Christianity] at least one aspect of what they term 'the Great Apostasy.'"[42]

Both the restored gospel and American culture contain strands that draw upon both a Hebrew and a Greek heritage. That helped me see why I had felt the conflicts I did in my student days. For example, most U.S. coins carry two familiar phrases: "Liberty" and "In God We Trust." The personal "liberty" of the individual was a key element in Greek values. To the Greeks, man was the measure of all things. For Socrates, nothing was more important than to "know thyself," and his ultimate goal was to ennoble man through reason.

But the coin's other phrase, "In God We Trust," would have perplexed an ancient Greek—even though it spoke directly to the Hebrew soul, who put his whole trust in God. The Hebrew pattern sought to glorify God, not man, and one reached this goal through faith and obedience, not through human reasoning. This

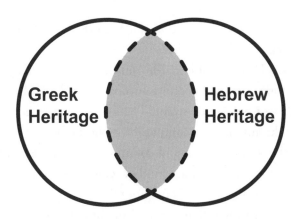

tiny comparison contains the seeds of countless arguments contrasting reason with faith.

The Restoration values both personal liberty and reason. No other religion or philosophy takes a higher view of man's nature and potential, as evidenced by such scriptures as "This is my work and my glory—to bring to pass the immortality and eternal life of man" (Moses 1:39) and "Man was also in the beginning with God" (D&C 93:29). Other scriptures stress the place of reason: "study it out in your mind" (D&C 9:8) and "all things denote there is a God" (Alma 30:44). And Elder John A. Widtsoe wrote an LDS book called *A Rational Theology*.

On the other hand, the Restoration teaches that all blessings are predicated on obedience (see D&C 130:20–21). Faith in God is both the first gospel principle and an essential check against unrestrained liberty and reason. When we disobey God, we not only reject divine authority, we disqualify ourselves from future blessings.

Note in the diagram above two circles that partially overlap each other. One circle represents the Greek tradition, with its emphasis on reason and individualism. The other circle represents the Hebrew tradition, with its emphasis on faith and authoritarianism. At the left end of the spectrum is the Greek tradition alone. At the right end is the Hebrew tradition alone. Inside the overlap, the two traditions can check each other.

We will be in trouble if the rigid authoritarianism of our Hebrew strain cuts itself completely loose from the anchoring reasonableness of our Greek strain. That's what happened with my former stake missionary companion—the Hebrew strain gone wild. Unchecked by reason and common sense, he veered off the right-hand edge and became a kind of "cultist Mormon."

Conversely, the bishop ran aground when he couldn't reason his way through the differences and the limitations he perceived among some Church leaders. His unchecked commitment to reason alone eventually took him out of the Church—the Greek strain gone wild. We could view those on this end of the spectrum as "cultural Mormons," accepting only that part of the gospel that meets their standard of rationality. So we can fall off the edge at either the right or left extreme—both potential responses to the complexity created by the tension between faith and reason.

The area of overlap, where individualistic and authoritarian principles coexist, offers a more productive perspective. Here both authoritarianism and individualism act as a check against each other. Both sets of principles are true, and both play a role in our decisions and attitudes—although varying circumstances may lead to different outcomes in particular cases. Similar check-and-balance interaction occurs between faith and reason, which both extend well into the area of overlap.

Within the overlap of our dual heritage, true principles drawn from both traditions can sometimes compete and conflict. For example, as noted earlier, "liberty" is in a natural tension with "in God we trust." If we trust in God, we will need to limit our liberty to the bounds He sets. And we know that Christ's teachings are full of similar paradoxes—true principles that seem to conflict but can be reconciled by higher doctrines. So West Belnap was right. We should nourish our religious commitments in both our hearts and our heads, even if that means we must also work through paradoxes.

I also found that the best way to resolve such tensions is not through abstract discussion, but through personal examples of real people—such as Elder Neal A. Maxwell, whose heart and head worked so well together. For instance, to encourage LDS professionals to contribute fully to the interests of both their disciplines and the Church, he said, "At BYU, we cannot let the world condemn our value system by calling attention to our professional mediocrity."[43] He also told BYU students and faculty to be unafraid of dealing with the world outside the Church, because the world needs them. He invited them to be like Joseph of Egypt. In today's spiritual famine, leaning into the fray and drawing on divine powers in their professional work allows them to become part of society's solutions, not just another hungry mouth to feed.

He urged them to take both scholarship and discipleship seriously, because faithful scholarship brings together both the life of the mind and the life of the spirit. At the same time, he believed that every dimension of the gospel was relevant to modern social problems and that, whenever possible, LDS scholars should take their research premises from gospel teachings.

Balance offers a helpful framework for resolving the tension between competing principles. We always stand better on two legs than one. But there is more. Now we need to ask what is beyond balance.

CHAPTER 7

Beyond Balance

When children first gain their balance, they are able to move, reach, and lift in coordinated ways not possible before. West Belnap helped solidify my understanding of the need for a heart-head balance. Then, as the years passed, I learned more about heavier moving, reaching, and lifting based on that balanced foundation. And I found myself entering another phase, which now looks like the simplicity beyond complexity.

For instance, I interviewed a prospective BYU faculty member who described his religious convictions as "an intelligent faith." At first blush, his attitude seemed balanced and constructive. But as I reflected more on his phrase, I began to wonder a little about modifying the word *faith* with a word like *intelligent*, because I could see that sometimes true, sacrificial faith needs to take us beyond where reason alone can go.

I recalled when President Marion G. Romney visited my mission in Germany. In a question-and-answer session, a missionary asked, "Why don't we baptize more *intelligent* people?" President Romney quoted D&C 93:36–37: "The glory of God is intelligence, or, in other words, light and truth. Light and truth forsake that evil one." Then he asked, "Does someone who joins the Church forsake evil and embrace light and truth?" The missionary nodded. President Romney asked, "So what kind of person is he?"

After a pause, the surprised missionary said, "An intelligent one?" President Romney said, "That's right. Next question."

I knew what was behind the missionary's question. I had also noticed that, with some important exceptions, we didn't attract a high percentage of our investigators from what might be called the German "intelligentsia." I've since realized that in the early history of this dispensation, as in biblical times, those drawn to the gospel's message were often described in scripture as "the weak and the simple" people of the earth (D&C 1:23). For "none is acceptable before God, save the meek and lowly of heart" (Moroni 7:44), and too often, when people "are learned they think they are wise, and they hearken not unto the counsel of God"—yet "to be learned is good if they hearken unto the counsels of God" (2 Nephi 9:28–29).

At about this same time, I watched a close friend my age decline physically from multiple sclerosis. He gradually lost his ability to walk, to stand, and then to sit. During the stage when he was fully bedridden, his wife passed away from cancer. His family wheeled him into her funeral on a hospital bed. Not long after his wife's funeral, we had a visit in his home. The more he talked, the more surprised I was at the spirit of peace and light that surrounded him. He said he couldn't stop thinking about how fortunate his life had been—so blessed by the woman he'd married, by the children the Lord had given them, by their rich life together in their wholesome little town. He chuckled as he said how glad he was now that he and his wife took so many "happily ever after" trips in their early years, even though they couldn't afford it.

He spoke of his admiration for the pioneers who left Nauvoo to settle Utah. He remembered that many of them were endowed in the Nauvoo Temple to strengthen them for their trek into the fearful wilderness. Every signal that came from him was authentic, and I sensed no self-pity. The light in his face and the spirit in the room told me that I was watching the sacred process of

sanctification, which his deteriorating physical condition paradox-
ically seemed to enhance.

That night I read D&C 101:2–5, "I, the Lord, have suffered
. . . affliction to come upon them, [and] those who will not endure chastening . . . *cannot* be sanctified" (emphasis added). The
meek and lowly simplicity we seek beyond complexity comes with
a price—though not always through physical suffering. Sacrifice
can take many forms, not all of them explainable fully by reason.

Then I watched our son Tom and his wife, Tracy, experience
the birth of a child who had severe cerebral palsy. Because this baby
had threatened to come early, Tracy had been on total bed rest
for nine weeks. Despite discomfort and medical warnings, she became very single-minded about keeping that pregnancy until the
baby could survive after birth. One night she sensed that somehow
her sacrifice emulated the Savior's example—giving up her body's
strength to strengthen another body. That thought helped her see
her experience as a privilege, not a burden.

They named their baby Chaya, which means "life" in Hebrew.
Chaya was never able to walk or talk or feed herself. But her smile
could light up a room. Early on, Tom gave Chaya a blessing in
which he recognized her birth as a defining event in her parents'
lives. He felt that God knew their circumstances and that this
child's condition had great purpose. Their family had been asked
to offer a sacrifice that would somehow make the Lord's own sacrifice more meaningful to them. Chaya eventually passed away at
age fifteen, but the convictions they felt from her father's blessing
continued to grow for her family.

Something about these two experiences set me to thinking
again about the meaning of "intelligent faith." The long, miserable
illnesses and then the deaths of both my friend and Chaya defied
rational explanation, and yet I had witnessed their sanctifying ef-
fects. I sensed that a balanced quest for knowledge, as valuable as

that is, perhaps can't be our ultimate end. Simply *knowing* something will not sanctify us; it won't make us capable of being in God's presence. And our sanctifying circumstances won't always be rational. By its very nature, faith ultimately takes us beyond the boundaries of reason. So if we condition our faith on rationality, we might shrink back from a sanctifying experience—and thus not discover what the experience could teach.

Still, even if yielding to such transforming experiences is necessarily a leap of faith, we can't go there until we've walked as far as the light of our search for knowledge allows. And a lifetime of trying to make sense of mortality, especially on days when it may not seem to make much sense, can give us the experience we need to appreciate the value of our sanctification.

In the balanced stance of accepting both the ideal and the real, we prize individualism and reason, yet we also prize our faith in God's authority. We would not return to a simplicity so innocent that it completely excludes either reason or faith. But the simplicity beyond complexity invites us to realize that a balanced approach alone won't be enough. When we are stretched to our extremities, we must reach for a new level that draws most deeply on our Hebrew roots.

No wonder Elder Maxwell said "we should have our citizenship in Jerusalem with a passport to Athens."[44] And part of the sacrifice the Lord may require is that we accept what He may "inflict" upon us (see Mosiah 3:19) without understanding to our rational satisfaction why we should be lost in some dark night of the soul. We can trust that eventually the light of Christ's atoning power will pierce our darkness and bless us with understanding.

Although he admired fine scholarship, Elder Maxwell believed that the life of a disciple-scholar is more about consecration than it is about scholarship. He did believe that faithful "scholarship [can be] a form of worship, another dimension of consecration." But he was concerned about scholars or students who measure and examine the gospel and the Church by what they have learned in their academic disciplines—more than they examine their disciplines through the lens of the gospel.

When Elder Maxwell first asked me to write his biography, I thought his life would focus on his contributions as a strong role model for educated Latter-day Saints. However, my research soon showed me that his life's core message was more about becoming a real disciple than it was about learning and scholarship. For example, his understanding of the word *disciple* developed over time. He first used the term in the 1960s as a synonym for *Church member*. Then, as Church Commissioner of Education in the early 1970s, he became concerned about the growing influence of modern secularism. He began using *disciple* to describe those Church members who resist secular siren calls. Later he came to know several Church members who were coping with adversity in ways that enhanced their spiritual growth. He soon felt that those people were the real disciples.

His call to the Quorum of the Twelve in 1981 nudged him to turn his full attention toward becoming a more faithful disciple of Christ himself. Reflecting his great determination to live better, his writing and his talks now focused more on the disciple's personal relationship with Christ and how the Lord will help us learn such Christlike attributes as patience, hope, and lowliness of heart. He also saw discipleship as more a process than a single choice, and he realized that the Lord sometimes uses adversity to teach His followers what they need to learn for their development.

That is why he wrote, in terms that would one day take on highly personal meaning for him, that "the very act of choosing to be a disciple can bring to us a certain special suffering. [Such] suffering and chastening is the dimension that comes with deep discipleship," when the Lord takes us "to the very edge of our faith;

[and] we teeter at the edge of our trust [in] a form of learning as it is administered at the hands of a loving Father."[45]

No wonder, then, that when his doctors told him in 1997 that, at age seventy, he had an aggressive form of leukemia, he said to his wife, Colleen, "I should have seen it coming." What did he mean? Neal Maxwell, the ardent student of discipleship, had signed up years earlier for divine tutoring, and his Tutor had admitted him to clinical graduate studies. In his remaining seven years, he wrapped his arms and his body around the heart-wrenching process of sanctification as his final tutorial.

Most people who experience a terminal illness can't help being consumed with their own suffering, but this was not true for Elder Maxwell. He saw himself in a time for testing and refining. And because he chose not to let his own misery imprison him, he could reflect on what his new understanding could teach him and how it helped him teach others. He sensed from a spiritual impression that the Lord had given him leukemia so that he "could teach the people with more authenticity."

As a result, those who had known him for years now saw a new mellowness, greater empathy, increased spiritual sensitivity, and keener compassion for other people's needs. Elder Maxwell viewed this experience as a gift, not as an achievement. He knew the Lord was giving him a new, sanctified heart filled with divine attributes, and he said, "The natural man's heart is pretty self-centered and hard." But "adversity can squeeze out of us the [remaining] hypocrisy that's there. [So for me] it's been a great spiritual adventure, one I would not want to have missed. And even though this has [had high costs], it's been a great blessing. I know people may think I'm just being patriotic to say that, but it's true."[46]

Somehow, watching Elder Maxwell's experience at close range, like watching the experience of my friend with M.S., helped change my perspective about my "religious problem." I was seeing beyond mere balance, feeling a heightened desire to develop the capacity to make sanctifying sacrifices. Those who desire sanctification must often pay a most demanding price, one that is beyond logical comprehension. Rather than looking for a rational explanation, Elder Maxwell would trustingly say he knew God loves us, but he didn't know the meaning of all things (see 1 Nephi 11:17).

Not long ago a student friend came by for a visit. A few months earlier, we had met his father in a hospital, where he was near the end of a terminal illness. Despite his tears and his questions, this father was full of peace and purpose. He said he knew his days were numbered, but he had accepted his stake president's challenge to read the scriptures and internalize all he could about the doctrine of sanctification. His countenance and his thoughts were similar to what I had seen before, with my friend and with Elder Maxwell. We offered words intended to encourage, but he was the one who gave *us* spiritual perspective.

His son had come to tell us that his father had just passed away. Then he said he had learned about sanctification from his father during his final weeks, and that had permanently changed his view of his daily life. Drawing on his father's experience, he said now he didn't want to wait until he had a terminal illness. He wanted to live in a better way *now*—closer to what he called "the things of eternity." This student's visit somehow illustrated the simplicity beyond complexity for us, even though he knew that he would probably need to pay his own high price and wade through more of his own personal complexity.

Something about the consecrated sacrifice of a broken heart and a contrite spirit blesses us with inner sight, taking us to a higher realm than mere balance can ever lift us—even though standing on that balanced foundation helps us reach upward. The simplicity beyond complexity doesn't ask us to give up anything of value in our reasoning, though it does recognize reason's limits.

Yet from this higher vantage point, we need even more rigorous inquiry, especially about nurturing the things of eternity.

At this level of maturing simplicity, being a true disciple is not so much about what one does or how one thinks, but about who and what one is—and is becoming. In the course of Elder Maxwell's adult life, he gradually shifted his emphasis from large-scale "macro" concerns about secularization and social problems to the more focused, personal "micro" concerns of how to live our lives. Not that the macro problems don't matter—he just knew that the micro problems are the ones we can do the most about. And in the long run, he knew that the gospel's way of changing the individual is the only lasting way to change society. As he put it, in the end there are no hyphenated words like *disciple-scholar*. If we are not finally true disciples, it won't matter much what else we are.

The painting below is a visual version of entering into the simplicity beyond complexity. It is Swiss painter Eugene Burnand's depiction of John and Peter, true disciples, running to the tomb very early on the first Easter morning. In John's words, "They *ran* both together" (John 20:4; emphasis added) until they reached the sepulchre.

These two faces capture the anxious tension between faith and reason. Since no one had ever risen from the dead, it would have been irrational for John and Peter to think that Christ could live again. No wonder they hadn't understood Him when He said He must soon leave them, yet in "a little while, and ye shall see me [and] your sorrow shall be turned into joy" (John 16:17–20). But their faces also show their faith and hope rising to overcome their rational fears. And when John and Peter eventually did meet the risen Lord, their having been faithful enough to run to Him hastened that ultimate resolution of their complexity.

This painting speaks to us about taking action, moving—now, early, as on Easter morning. We don't need to wait until we have a terminal disease to get serious about the things of eternity. We can feel *now* the excitement of quickening our step as we run to meet Him. And we can hasten our desire to live closer now to that eternal Presence, so He can better prepare us for whatever further sanctifying complexity awaits us.

CHAPTER 8

When Do the Angels Come?

The veil between heaven and earth usually hides the Lord and His angels from our sight. Yet during the early stages of our spiritual development, we may experience unmistakable moments when the veil is especially thin, moving our sense of belief to a feeling of certainty: "O then, is not this real?" we ask. And Alma replies, "Yea, because it is light; and . . . it is discernible" (Alma 32:35). Yet our discerning this light does not yield a perfect knowledge. We must nourish the tree of faith to "get root" against the day "when the heat of the sun . . . scorcheth it" (Alma 32:37–38). As we wait and work for more light, our days of searching can last many years.

Our sense of the unseen world increases through our early conversion experiences, missionary service, attending college, or falling in love. We can compare these crucial, formative periods of spiritual breakthrough with the Kirtland Temple dedication season in Church history and compare our later years with the Nauvoo Temple dedication season—and beyond. This comparison will illustrate our now-familiar pattern: from simplicity to complexity to the simplicity beyond complexity.

The Kirtland (1830–1838) and Nauvoo (1839–1846) periods of Church history were each filled with a distinctive blend of astounding blessings and chilling opposition. We focus here on the specific season of the temple dedication in each city.

The early Kirtland years were unusually happy ones for Joseph Smith and the Saints. Wonderful events had blessed them in only a few years—the vision in the grove, the publication of the Book of Mormon, the organization of the Church, the optimistic launching of missionary work, the School of the Prophets, and mighty revelations outlining a glorious future. It was a youthful, buoyant time. The Saints had barely begun to sense what could yet await them, coiled like a deadly snake, just around the corner of history: mobs, persecution, apostasy, and martyrdom.

But first the angels came. Indeed, the dedication of the Kirtland Temple in March of 1836 was probably the greatest single spiritual outpouring in modern Church history. Joseph wrote that just after the dedicatory prayer, "Frederick G. Williams arose and testified that [during the prayer] an angel entered the window and took his seat between Father Smith and himself. David Whitmer also saw angels in the house."[47]

Later, "Brother George A. Smith arose and began to prophesy, when a noise was heard like the sound of a rushing mighty wind, which filled the Temple, and all the congregation simultaneously arose, being moved upon by an invisible power; many began to speak in tongues and prophesy; . . . and I beheld that the Temple was filled with angels. . . . The people of the neighborhood came running together (hearing an unusual sound within, and seeing a bright light like a pillar of fire resting upon the Temple,) and were astonished at what was taking place."[48]

Joseph said that at a concluding meeting, "The Savior made his appearance to some, while angels ministered to others, and it was a Pentecost and an endowment indeed, long to be remembered, for the sound shall go forth from this place into all the world, and occurrences of this day shall be handed down upon the pages of sacred history, to all generations."[49]

Now contrast those glorious experiences with the dreadful conditions surrounding the Nauvoo Temple dedication just nine years later. Joseph and Hyrum had been slain. The Church was racked with dissension and apostasy, and the dark spirit of the martyrdom hovered over Nauvoo like the destroying angel of death. The Saints knew they couldn't stay. They worked frantically to finish the temple, even as they also prepared for their fearful westward trek.

Part of the Nauvoo Temple was dedicated in October 1845, even before the building was finished, and in December Brigham Young began to administer the temple ordinances day and night. Within two months, the first company of wagons crossed the frozen Mississippi, never to return.

The story is told of a blind convert named Brother Williams who came from Massachusetts to Nauvoo in time to help complete the temple. Brother Williams had heard the stories of Kirtland, and he believed fervently that when the Nauvoo Temple was dedicated, the Savior and even the resurrected Joseph would return. He anticipated great spiritual manifestations that would heal his blindness. He believed that each stone they were laying brought him one step closer to the Savior's healing hand. But the Nauvoo Temple dedication was no Kirtland. There were no recorded visible manifestations, no angelic ministries, no Pentecost.

Our youthful years as missionaries and students are, despite their typical growing pains, frequently a kind of Kirtland for us: a simple and beautiful time, filled with intellectual breakthroughs, private spiritual moments, and emerging idealistic convictions. Those years may lift us for a time above the noise and confusion of worldly valleys to a high mountain peak, where we develop a growing closeness to the Infinite. But the day of complexity always seems to come—the day when we must descend our mountains, must leave our Kirtlands.

When we do, sooner or later, we may have our own disruptive kind of Nauvoo, perhaps more than once. We will have our own frozen rivers and parched deserts to cross, a moral or intellectual or spiritual wilderness to tame. Perhaps we will feel bewildered and disappointed, and we may look back longingly, wondering how to recapture our youthful Kirtland years.

When our Nauvoo comes, we might feel the waning of our sense of spiritual wonder, as the accumulating pressures and pollutions of life seem to cast doubt on the reality of inspiration or the worth of the institutional Church or the value of giving ourselves unselfishly to others. Some of our friends, or some of our foes, may alarm us with reports that this or that element of Church history or doctrine isn't what we thought it was.

When our Nauvoo comes, we may find ourselves living in a culture that offers little reinforcement for our belief in the ideals of family life. The surrounding environment may attack our devotion to marriage and children. Some of us may begin to feel a growing sense of distance in our marriages as those around us take for granted that modern men and women should not feel bound by unconditional family commitments. But we will know better, for we lived once in Kirtland, where the Spirit whispered to us that the doctrine is true: marriage is sacred and love is forever.

When our Nauvoo comes, we might turn away in sadness, feeling that perhaps our earlier Kirtland-like moments must not have been what we thought they were. "How could those stories be true?" some will ask. "We see no angels here, not now, when we need them most. What happened at Kirtland must have been the foolish imagination of our youth." We may feel pressure to see things this way, perhaps surrounded by those who whisper tauntingly in our ears as did the enemy in Nauvoo: "Your Prophet is dead. Wake up—it was all a childhood dream."

When our Nauvoo comes, it will neither surprise us nor throw us off course if we have kept the image of Kirtland burning brightly in our memories. It is all right, we will say, we understand. "Ye cannot behold with your natural eyes . . . the design of your God concerning those things which shall come hereafter. . . . For after much tribulation come the blessings" (D&C 58:3–4). A new and deeper simplicity—that for which we long—can come to us only after our season of complexity.

So we will pick up our wagons and our families and head west. As we do, we will sense that Kirtland was given to us as a first witness, to be told to our children and their children's children, that they may know that God is the Lord. He slumbers not nor sleeps. We will know that, always, for we were there for that joyful season in the Kirtland village.

We still think of Brother Williams, his blind eyes glistening with hope, waiting for Jesus and His angels to come to the Nauvoo Temple. We don't know what happened to him after Nauvoo. Did he find the healing he hungered for? Did he find his Savior and see the face of Brother Joseph? We suppose that he and the other faithful ones did find the enlightenment and the peace they sought—but later, perhaps within the last wagon along some dreary prairie trail, or in struggling to build a new life, far away in the West.

We suppose that Brother Williams made the same discovery as did the Saints in the Martin and Willie handcart companies, who were trapped by heavy, early snows on the high plains of Wyoming. One survivor said they "came through with the absolute knowledge that God lives, for we became acquainted with him in our extremities." Many times, he continued, when he was "so weak and weary from illness and lack of food that I could hardly put one foot ahead of the other," he began to feel that the handcart was pushing him. But whenever he looked back "to see who was pushing my cart, . . . my eyes saw no one. I knew then that the angels of God were there."[50]

Such unseen angelic manifestations in the extremities of our lives will probably have more profound meaning to us than the more visible outpouring of our Kirtlands. The Lord has promised that if we are true and faithful, He Himself may be "in your midst and ye cannot see me" (D&C 38:7). Even if we do not see Him, He can "be on your right hand and on your left, and [His] Spirit shall be in your hearts," and the angels who came to Kirtland will be "round about you, to bear you up" (D&C 84:88).

Moreover, our memories of Kirtland can be enriched by our later, perhaps more turbulent, experience. The very meaning of our earlier witnesses will grow richer with the perspective of both time and complexity. We ventured to Nauvoo because of what we saw in Kirtland. That we once saw so clearly is our witness that we can again see clearly, now with even greater depth, in the very midst of—or perhaps because of—our afflictions.

After all, the angels *are* there. And someday, perhaps not so far away in time or space, we might be prepared enough and have reason enough to see the angels of Kirtland once more. The conditions on which our vision may pierce the veil are not fully known to us. Those conditions aren't always known even to the prophets.

When Elijah was about to be taken from the earth, Elisha asked that a double portion of Elijah's spirit might remain with him. Elijah replied that this was "a hard thing: nevertheless, if thou see me when I am taken from thee, it shall be so unto thee; but if not, it shall not be so." Suddenly, flaming horses and a chariot of fire appeared and took Elijah by a whirlwind into heaven. And the Lord granted the desire of Elisha's heart, for his eyesight pierced the veil: "And Elisha saw [the angels], and he cried, My father, my father, the chariot of Israel, and the horsemen thereof" (2 Kings 2:9–12).

Who are those horsemen? When do they come and where do they go? They must not be far away, for they have come again in the modern age. Not long before the dedication of the Kirtland Temple, Joseph Smith's scribe saw "in a vision the armies of heaven protecting the saints in their return to Zion."[51] The next day, "the heavens were opened upon elder Sylvester Smith, and he leaping up exclaimed, 'The horsemen of Israel and the chariots thereof.'"[52]

Whoever they are, the horsemen of Israel still watch over the Saints with such care that we can know of a surety, "They that be with us are more than they that be with them." The mountain might even be "full of horses and chariots of fire" (2 Kings 6:16–17).

From the stories of Kirtland, we know that the angels come to celebrate and bear unforgettable witness in the formation of our faith, even if we need to wait for further visible witnesses until our faith has been tried, enriched, and deepened by the fires of complexity. "When through fiery trials thy pathway shall lie, My grace, all sufficient, shall be thy supply. The flame shall not hurt thee; I only design Thy dross to consume and thy gold to refine."[53] Thus do we move into the calm, mature, deeply rooted simplicity on the other side of complexity.

CHAPTER 9

The Value of the Veil

Some people who wonder if they are losing their religious faith say not only that they are losing confidence in Joseph and the Restoration, but that they are losing confidence in the very existence of God—implying that if the Restoration isn't true, no other religious explanation of life could be true either. And suddenly agnosticism or even atheism sounds like a real option to them.

That can be seen as a backhanded compliment to the strength of the Restoration's claims. Yet those whose faith has been that deeply shaken might actually be asking themselves for the first time how we can "know" anything about spiritual realities beyond what we can prove with our rational senses. One friend was talking with some coworkers who said they were atheists. When he asked why they didn't believe God exists, they said, "No one ever comes back to life. What convinces you that Jesus did when no else does?" Our friend wanted to "give . . . a reason of the hope that is in you" (1 Peter 3:15), but he couldn't think of a "substantial reason, and for the first time truly questioned the religion of my childhood."

He might have mentioned the Bible verses and modern scriptures that offer eyewitness accounts that both Jesus and many others "came back to life"—that's partly why the Book of Mormon is called "another witness of Jesus Christ." But in the moment, what perhaps caught him so fully off guard was his sense that he couldn't offer "a substantial [enough] *reason*" that might convince his friends.

A theistic explanation for life actually makes more sense than does an atheistic explanation. What are the odds that a tornado spinning through a junkyard would create a flyable Boeing 747? Or, as Alma told the skeptical Korihor, "All things denote there is a God; yea, even the earth, and all things that are upon the face of it, yea, and its motion" (Alma 30:44).

Biologist Francis Collins led the international project in the year 2000 that put together the first complete map of the entire human DNA code. Seeing that complex code as "the language in which God created life," Collins writes that "belief in God can be an entirely rational choice, and . . . the principles of faith are . . . complementary with the principles of science." In fact, the earth contains in exactly the right proportions *all* of the fifteen scientific "physical constants" that are each crucial to sustaining the planet's complex life forms. The likelihood that this unique combination could come together by sheer chance "is almost infinitesimal. [Without God] our universe is [so] wildly improbable [that] faith in God [is] more rational than disbelief."[54]

At the same time, Collins is talking about probabilities, not absolute scientific certainties. And God has some good reasons for making it so difficult for us to "prove" religious realities beyond question, including the reality of His own existence. That's not to say He has left us without evidence, witnesses, and probabilities. Still, there may be times when it seems that He has left us in the dark. Even Joseph Smith cried out in Liberty Jail, "O God, where art thou? And where is the pavilion that covereth thy hiding place?" (D&C 121:1).

Joseph was discovering what Job had also learned the hard way: "Behold, I go forward, but he is not there; and backward, but I cannot perceive him: On the left hand, where he doth work, but

I cannot behold him: he hideth himself on the right hand, that I cannot see him: But he knoweth the way that I take: when he hath tried me, I shall come forth as gold" (Job 23:8–10).

Let us consider, then, the value of the veil that covers God's hiding place—the same veil that blocks our memories of our pre-earth life. In the Kirtland Temple, Joseph Smith said, "The veil was taken from our minds, and the eyes of our understanding were opened" (D&C 110:1). Before the brother of Jared beheld the premortal Christ, "the veil was taken from off [his] eyes" (Ether 3:6). Indeed, there have been "many" of such strong faith that they "could not be kept from within the veil, but truly saw with their eyes [what] they had beheld with an eye of faith" (Ether 12:19). Yet for the most part, the rest of us still see with the eye of faith—a faith that is not blind, yet remains subject to the veil.

Not only does the veil keep us from remembering our premortal past, it also keeps us from seeing many things that are going on at the present. God and His angels almost always stay in their hiding places—except on those exquisitely rare occasions when He does part that veil.

After the Savior's Resurrection, for example, He saw and talked with two of His disciples on the road to Emmaus. They didn't recognize Him. When He heard their disappointment about this Jesus in whom they had "trusted" (note the past tense), He saw that they had missed the core message of His mortal ministry. So, "Beginning at Moses . . . he expounded unto them in all the scriptures the things concerning himself" (see Luke 24:13–31). He didn't say who He was. He taught them exactly what He'd taught them while in the flesh. Only later did they recognize Him. Why didn't He tell them sooner?

When a rich man died about the same time as did Lazarus, the rich man pleaded with father Abraham to send Lazarus back to teach the rich man's family: "If one went unto them from the dead, they will repent." But Abraham replied, "If they hear not Moses and the prophets, neither will they be persuaded, though one rose from the dead" (Luke 16:30–31). Why not?

Christ was the life and the light of men, a light that "shineth in darkness; and the darkness comprehended it not" (John 1:5). He came into the world, but His own received Him not. If it is eternal life to know God, why didn't He reveal Christ more obviously? He came so privately, so unobtrusively. God could send a great chariot across the sky every day at noon, drawn by flying white horses. The chariot could stop right above the earth—just like a sudden, total eclipse of the sun—and a voice from the great beyond could say, "And now a word from our Creator." Why doesn't He do things like that?

Learning from *experience* teaches us in ways nothing else can. In designing His plan for our mortal experience, God consciously took the risk that some of His children wouldn't come back. Didn't He have the power to touch us with some kind of wand that would give us the capacity to live with Him in the celestial kingdom?

Even the Savior had to undergo the trials of mortality—without shortcuts. He "offered up prayers and supplications with strong crying and tears unto him who was able to save him from death; . . . Though he were a Son, yet *learned* he obedience by the things which he suffered" (Hebrews 5:7–8; emphasis added). So it is with us. We need milk before we're ready for meat. "For every one that useth milk is unskilful in the word of righteousness: for he is a babe. But strong meat belongeth to them that are of full age, even those who *by reason of use* have their senses exercised to discern both good and evil" (Hebrews 5:13–14; emphasis added). Only "by reason of use" can we exercise our senses to truly understand both good and evil. What is it about experience that is so essential it's worth the risk that we may not come back?

Salvation and exaltation are not just abstract goals. Those terms describe an entire process that requires growth, development, and change. Central to that growth process is mortality's unique opportunity to let us learn by experience—by practice—which is the only way we can develop capacities and skills. We're not here just to learn facts and absorb information. There is something about forcing people to be righteous that interferes with, even prohibits, the process that righteousness in a free environment is designed to enable. Righteous living causes something to happen to people.

There are two very different kinds of knowledge. One involves such rational processes as gathering information and memorizing. The other kind of knowledge we might call skill development—like learning how to play the piano or swim or take a computer apart, learning to sing or dance or think. The process of becoming Christlike is more about acquiring skills than it is about learning facts and figures. And the only way to develop those divine skills is by living His teachings. Even God can't teach us those skills unless we participate fully in the process, with all the trials and all the errors that are inherent in learning a skill by practice.

What coach could improve an athlete's skills without supervising his or her trials and errors? What piano teacher could teach students to play if they don't practice? The "think method," in which young musicians were encouraged to learn to play their instruments solely by "thinking" of the music, sounded appealing in *The Music Man*, but it goes only so far. When the first graduate of the "Do It without Practice Piano Course" walks onto the stage of Carnegie Hall to play a piano concerto with a waiting orchestra, what do you suppose will happen? Not much. Why? Some things can be learned only by practice.

European scholar Michael Polanyi has identified "skills" as a unique field of knowledge.[55] He writes that often the essence of a skill can't adequately be described, measured, or specified. So the skill can't be transmitted by written descriptions and instructions intended to be memorized by later generations. *"It can be passed on only by example from master to apprentice."* Therefore, "an art which has fallen into disuse for the period of a generation is altogether lost" and "these losses are usually irretrievable. It is pathetic to watch the endless efforts—equipped with microscopy and chemistry, with mathematics and electronics—to reproduce a single violin of the kind the half-literate Stradivarius turned out as a matter of routine more than 200 years ago."[56]

It follows, then, that we can learn a skill only by imitating the skillful performance of one who has mastered the skill—even when the teacher whom we imitate cannot specify every detail of the art. There is a close analogy between this fact and the central gospel concept that emulating the Savior's example is the ultimate way of internalizing the gospel, a way that transcends merely following specific commandments and detailed doctrines. Again Polanyi:

"To learn by example is to submit to authority. You follow your master because you trust his manner of doing things even when you cannot analyse and account in detail for its effectiveness. By watching the master and emulating his efforts in the presence of his example, the apprentice unconsciously picks up the rules of the art, including those which are not explicitly known to the master himself. These hidden rules can be assimilated only by a person who surrenders himself to that extent uncritically to the imitation of another. A society which wants to preserve a fund of personal knowledge must submit to tradition."[57]

Many people don't want to test the gospel's truth because they aren't willing to submit to the Lord's guidance. We can plead with the skeptics to just try Alma's experiment and see, but they often want us to "prove" the faith proposition before they will submit themselves in ways that seem to them a loss of their freedom. And if they doubt that the process of living the Savior's teachings really will bear fruit, their own doubts become a self-fulfilling prophecy—*no faith, no fruit.* Unless they yield, participate, and lose themselves in the faith process, they won't taste the fruit from the tree of life. Without total immersion, the skill will always elude them.

A blind person who successfully uses a walking stick has learned to "see" with the stick. But that person can't fully describe to anyone else, including another blind person, exactly what the stick is telling him or her. Those who just close their eyes for a while to see what blindness is like aren't motivated to exert themselves at a deep enough level to learn what the stick can tell them. Why not? *Because unless you are blind, you don't have to know.* The blind person must be willing to practice with the cane, with all the mistakes that inevitably go with practice. And practice isn't just repetition—it requires repeated effort aimed at learning a specific skill and learning from mistakes, in the pursuit of specific growth.[58]

How does one help others see that? Our skeptical friends might say, "What is so great about the celestial kingdom? Explain it to me so I can understand it, and then maybe I can put up with all the commandments, submit myself to the Master, and go through all the practice and routine. But first, prove to me that it will all be worthwhile in the end." What can we say?

It often helps to bear a personal, experience-based testimony or to offer role models whose examples show what the developing skill looks like, even with all the messiness and mistakes of trial-and-error practice. But ultimately, human minds, resurrected or not, can't communicate fully to other human minds what the developed fruits of faith really taste like. Each person just needs to trust, plant the seed, and try the process with all of its required discipline. Something will happen to one who honestly tries, and thereby *discovers* that a core purpose of our mortality is the opportunity to develop the skills, the capacities, that are necessary for us to live in the celestial kingdom.

A six-year-old child lacks the mental and physical capacity to drive a car. Until he or she is developmentally ready to learn the required skill and judgment, driving on a freeway will likely destroy the child—and others. The same is true of our premature introduction to the freedom—and the responsibility—of living in a kingdom governed by celestial laws. That opportunity can be liberating or crushing, depending upon our preparation to receive it.

The Lord said that "whatever principle of intelligence we attain unto in this life, it will rise with us in the resurrection" (D&C 130:18). "Principle of intelligence" may refer to facts, information, and the laws of the universe. But it especially refers to Christlike capacity and skills like self-control, obedience, compassion, patience, and unselfishness. Why would we be damned if we saw a sign—if the veil were parted too early? We would be stopping our progress. Even if a chariot were to fly visibly across the sky every day, seeing such wonders would not help us really to know the Father and the Son. Eternal life—knowing Them—is a quality of life, the fruit of the long-term, difficult, gradual development of the capacity to become as Christ is. When we begin to live as He does, we will begin to know Him.

The idea that exaltation results from a process of skill development may help explain why there is a veil. Faith and repentance and knowing God are processes and principles of action, understood not only by defining them but by experiencing them. God is a great teacher, and He knows the patterns and the principles we must follow—and practice—in order to develop divine capacities. He can teach us those skills, but only if we submit to His tutoring.

Much of the substance of Christ's gospel can't be fully measured; it can't all be specified, except as it is understood by experience. But that is no reason to value it less. We can't totally explain our most significant experiences—our love for our families, our testimonies, our feelings of gratitude for the Lord's love and mercy. To reduce these essences to a content that we can communicate fully to other people may diminish their sacredness. Like beauty and joy, they are too important, too nuanced, to be totally specifiable.

There is a veil between our world of mortality and God's world of the eternities. It can become very thin at times. But for most of us the veil remains, for He has placed it there to help us learn how we must live, and who we must become, to live with Him someday.

CHAPTER 10

Choosing to Believe

One late summer afternoon when our family was visiting relatives in a distant city, our four-year-old son, Tom, disappeared without warning from a large city park. We made an extensive search of the entire area, ultimately involving the police as well as many neighbors. Then darkness came, and we were feeling frantic.

We gathered our children together and knelt in prayer. Among other things, we prayed that Tom might approach someone safe who would contact the police so they could call us. A short time later, the police called to report that they had found him, almost exactly as we had requested in the prayer. Before long a police car drove up with its red light circling and its wide-eyed cargo a bit shaken, but intact—wearing a big paper badge on his shirt: "Good buddy of the San Diego Police Department."

Later that night Tom's older brother said, "Dad, that was kind of magic, sort of, wasn't it?" We decided that it wasn't magic, but that the Lord had answered our prayer. Would Tom have turned up anyway? We don't know. But our family chose to believe that the prayer made a difference.

I once heard a university student tell his elders quorum what happened just after he was ordained a deacon. He lived on a farm, and his parents had promised him that a calf about to be born would be his very own to raise—his first. One morning when his parents were away, he was working in the barn when the expectant cow began to calve prematurely. In wonder, he watched the little calf's birth. Then suddenly the cow began to roll all over the calf—and he realized she was trying to kill it. He cried out to the Lord for help.

Not thinking about how much more the cow weighed than he did, he pushed on her with all his strength and somehow moved her away. He picked up the lifeless-looking calf in his arms and looked at it, the tears running down his cheeks. Then he remembered that he had every right to ask for the Lord's help. So he prayed again from the depths of his boyish, believing heart. Before long the little animal began to move and breathe normally. He knew his prayer had been heard.

Then the tears welled up in his eyes and he said, "Brethren, I tell you that story because I don't think I would do now what I did then. Now that I am older and less naïve, I 'know better' than to expect the Lord's help in a situation like that. If I relived that experience now, I'd probably believe it was a coincidence. I'm not sure how I've changed, but I may have lost something valuable." He felt less childlike, less believing.

What does it mean to "be believing"? And why does the Lord ask us to be that way?

Moroni wrote: "And who shall say that Jesus Christ did not do many mighty miracles? . . . and he ceaseth not to be God, and is a God of miracles. . . . Doubt not, but *be believing*" (Mormon 9:18–19, 27; emphasis added). And the Lord said, "Search diligently, pray always, and *be believing*, and all things shall work together for your good" (D&C 90:24; emphasis added).

The risen Lord counseled Thomas to "reach hither thy hand, and thrust it into my side: and be not faithless, but *believing*"

(John 20:27; emphasis added). Even after the doubter saw and felt the wounds, to be a true witness, he still needed to "be believing."

The act of believing originates in the heart of the beholder. The Savior said to those around Him, "He that hath ears to hear, let him hear" (Luke 8:8). Yet few of His listeners really understood His parables or perceived His miracles. It isn't easy to know which influences have a divine origin. Those who watched Jesus heal the sick faced the same question we do today when someone testifies that a priesthood blessing brought healing. Was it really a healing, or would the person have recovered anyway? Did the Lord really help our family find Tom? Did He bless that twelve-year-old with added strength to move the cow and then help the calf recover?

Even the matter of God's existence can sometimes seem to be a close question. With the unspeakable tragedies and misery we see throughout history and now all around us, some say there couldn't be a God. Others say that the order in nature could never have been accidental. Neither side can persuade the other on the basis of external evidence alone. Could it be that the Lord planned it that way—so that we are not forced by the circumstances to believe? There are so many things He could do to rend the veil. But "we walk by faith, not by sight" (2 Corinthians 5:7).

All four of Lehi's sons were born of the same goodly parents. The difference between the believers and unbelievers was not so much in what happened to them, but in their *attitude* toward what happened. That attitude originated within their own hearts, with each making his own free choice to be believing—or not.

When Nephi desired to see his father's dream, the Spirit answered, "Believest thou that thy father saw the tree of which he hath spoken?" Nephi said, "Yea . . . I believe all the words of my father." The Spirit then *rejoiced*, because he knew that only if Nephi had a believing attitude could the Spirit teach him. "Blessed art thou, Nephi, because thou believest in the Son of the most high

God; *wherefore*, thou shalt behold the things which thou hast desired" (1 Nephi 11:4–6; emphasis added).

Because he believed, then, Nephi saw the dream—but only a step at a time. The Spirit repeatedly stopped and asked what else he desired, what he understood. Then, when Nephi was "getting it," the Spirit would say again and again, "Look!" And each time, Nephi looked—and gradually understood: the city, the virgin, the child, until the angel asked, "Knowest thou the meaning of the tree which thy father saw?" Nephi could now respond, "Yea, it is the love of God . . . and I beheld the Son of God going forth" (1 Nephi 11:21–22, 24).

Instead of *telling* or *showing* Nephi the entire vision at once, the Spirit led him—one question at a time—helping him *discover* for himself each scene and what it meant. If the Spirit had just told him everything, Nephi wouldn't have grasped its full meaning. If Nephi hadn't chosen to believe, it's not just that the Spirit *wouldn't* show him the dream and tell him its meaning, but that He *couldn't* show him in a way Nephi would fully understand.

We value what we discover more than we value what we are told. And unless we discover God's influence for ourselves, perhaps we won't know it's there, even if an angel tells us it is. In Jacob's dream about the ladder reaching to heaven, with angels ascending and descending it, he saw God standing at the top of the ladder saying, "I am with thee, and will keep thee in all places whither thou goest." And then Jacob awoke and said, "Surely the Lord is in this place; and I knew it not" (Genesis 28:15–16).

Christ came to earth so quietly, so peacefully—a light that "shineth in darkness; and the darkness comprehended it not. . . . *But as many as received him, to them gave he power* to become the sons of God, even to them that believe on his name" (John 1:5, 12; emphasis added). It was all part of a plan carefully designed not to compel belief.

Jesus gave us other clues about the deliberateness of that plan. Frequently He told those who were blessed by a miracle to "tell no man what was done" (Luke 8:56; see also Matthew 8:4). One essential element in His plan is the principle of line upon line, precept upon precept (see Isaiah 28:10). Not only does He leave to us the initiative to believe, He imparts to His hearers only what they are ready to hear. Milk comes before meat. "I have yet many things to say unto you, but ye cannot bear them now" (John 16:12). So it was with the Spirit and Nephi.

Scholars in the philosophy of knowledge tell us that people tend to see what they want to see, especially when the evidence is ambiguous. "Confirmation bias," for example, is the human "tendency to interpret new evidence as [a] confirmation of one's existing beliefs or theories."[59] Perhaps that is why the mists of darkness in Lehi's dream describe the conditions of mortality so well. God has left us free, amid circumstances that do not compel our belief, to choose for ourselves, as an act of will, whether to grasp the iron rod in the midst of the darkness.

The significance of this "will to believe" applies to all human knowledge and experience, not just to religious experience. The influential American psychologist William James said, "The question of having moral beliefs is decided by our *will*. If your heart does not *want* a world of moral reality, your head will assuredly never make you believe in one."[60]

Our freely chosen willingness to believe may well be the determining factor in whether God's promises to us can be fulfilled—because our beliefs impel the actions that only we can take to nourish the seed of faith in its growth. It is God's work and His glory to help us enjoy eternal life (see Moses 1:39), but if we "neglect the tree [of eternal life] and take no thought for its nourishment," no matter how good the seed or how sweet the fruit, we "*cannot* have the fruit thereof" (Alma 32:38–39; emphasis added). If we deny ourselves that blessing, we not only short-circuit our own possi-bilities, we also frustrate God's desires to bless us. For, as William James put it, "God himself . . . may draw vital strength and in-crease of very being from our fidelity."[61]

James also said that the agnostic attitude—delaying decisions about issues of faith until we have more evidence—is, as a practical matter, impossible:

"Belief and doubt are living attitudes, and involve conduct on our part. . . . If I doubt that you are worthy of my confidence, I keep you uninformed . . . as if you were *un*worthy of the same. If I doubt the need of insuring my house, I leave it uninsured as . . . if I believed there were no need. [At such times] inaction [counts] as action, and when not to be *for* is to be practically *against*; [here] neutrality is . . . unattainable."[62]

Since our own attitudes and choices have so much influence on the outcomes of our life experience, James believed that whether life is worth living "depends on the liver"—that is, on who is liv-ing it. This is because "optimism and pessimism are definitions of the world," and our own reactions to the world often determine which definition is correct. Because the way life treats us depends so much on how we treat life, we are constantly at the mercy of our own choices—perhaps without realizing how much our own solitary choice can protect us or harm us.

"Not a victory is gained, not a deed of faithfulness or courage is done, except upon a *maybe*; not a service, . . . not a scientific exploration or experiment or textbook, that may not be a mistake. . . . [O]nly by risking our persons from one hour to another [do] we live at all. And often enough our faith beforehand in an uncer-tified result is the only thing that makes the result come true."[63]

Suppose you are climbing a mountain, writes James, and at one point your only escape is to leap across a deep chasm. "Have faith that you can" make the terrible leap, "and your feet are nerved to its accomplishment. But mistrust yourself . . . and you will hesitate [until] all unstrung and trembling . . . you roll into the abyss. Refuse to believe, and you shall indeed be right," for you will perish. "But believe, and again you shall be right, for you shall save yourself. You make one or the other of two possible universes true by your trust or mistrust—both universes having been only *maybes*" before you made your choice.[64]

Thus our faith in the unseen world strengthens us to do what *only we* can do to allow God's promises to take root, sprout, bud, and blossom in our lives. Unless we trust Him enough to act, God's promises to us remain as unfulfilled as if they did not exist. For example, unless we choose to exercise faith and repentance, we are as lost as if Christ had made no Atonement. "He that persists in . . . the ways of sin . . . remaineth in his fallen state [and] is as though there was no redemption made" (Mosiah 16:5). Conversely, only our willingness to *choose belief* and *choose trust* allows God to influence our lives to yield our most hoped-for outcomes: "Whoso putteth his trust in the Lord shall be safe" (Proverbs 29:25) and "shall be supported in their trials, and their troubles, and their afflictions" (Alma 36:3).

Viktor Frankl was an Austrian psychiatrist who survived years of unspeakable trauma in Nazi concentration camps, constantly watching his fellow inmates waste away and die—or be killed. His book *Man's Search for Meaning* recounts how the sheer brutality of his experience helped him discover ways to find meaning in life's most tragic circumstances—and therefore how to discover life's meaning (and a desire to keep living) in any circumstance.

For example, Frankl wrote, "Those who have a 'why' to live [for], can bear with almost any 'how.'"[65] "It [does] not really matter what we [expect] from life, but rather what life [expects] from us."[66] "The last of the human freedoms [is] to choose one's attitude in any given set of circumstances."[67] Therefore, "the meaning of life is to give life meaning."[68]

In providing a larger context for these piercing directives to *choose to believe that life is worth living*, Frankl writes as if he had been invited to comment on our earlier description of "the gap" between the real and the ideal, between what is and what ought to be: "Mental health is based on [the] tension . . . between what one has already achieved and what one still ought to accomplish, or *the gap between what one is and what one should become*. [This inherent] tension is . . . indispensable to mental well-being." Therefore we should challenge ourselves to exert our own "*will to meaning*," rather than seeking the comfort of "a tensionless state." The tension between the real and the ideal is not a threat to our safety but is "the call of a potential meaning waiting to be fulfilled."[69]

Frankl urges us to "strive and struggle" and exert our own "will to meaning" as we choose to believe that life is worth living. As we thus reach across "the gap," God will take us by the hand and invite us into the secure arms of His love. There we will know the new simplicity of just being "home" again. But, unlike the unaware infant in his or her mother's arms, through our striving and struggling we will have paid the price to *understand* where we are, who we are, and what it means to be at home with God.

Why is mortality structured this way? The Lord is very close to us. He even tells us, "Mine eyes are upon you. I am in your midst and ye cannot see me" (D&C 38:7). Yet He deliberately refrains from interfering with our agency and initiative. He just says, "be believing" and "be faithful," and "all things will work together for our good" (see Romans 8:28).

There is a profound difference between the person "that *saith* unto me, Lord, Lord," and the person who "*doeth the will* of my Father which is in heaven" (Matthew 7:21; emphasis added). Something happens to people who receive Him, who believe enough to do His will. For one thing, they learn for themselves that His doctrine is true: "If any man will do his will, he shall know of the doctrine, whether it be of God, or whether I speak of myself" (John 7:17). Further, some may say, "I don't believe that because I can't understand it." But believing precedes understanding. Understanding does not precede believing: "Because of their unbelief they could not understand the word of God" (Mosiah 26:3).

Beyond that, believers who "receive Him" gradually develop Christlike capacities and skills that other people don't stretch toward. Following His will changes them. Those who seek, or even find, a sign don't usually experience such changes, because actual changes in character and spirit depend on our active, voluntary participation. So by being believing, by receiving the Lord, and by following Him, the process of becoming like Him is set into motion.

The Lord really can't save us without our freely chosen initiative, energy, desires, and wholehearted *participation*. You can lead a horse to water, but you can't make him drink it. You can lead a child to a book, but you can't make her read it. The Savior offers the grace of His saving and exalting blessings only as we *willingly participate* in our own deliverance by choosing to believe Him, then by exerting all our strength to follow Him. This voluntary, active participation is essential to the growth process that results in our personal and spiritual development.

George Eliot wrote about the famous violin maker Antonio Stradivari, "'tis God gives skill, but not without men's hand: He could not make Antonio Stradivari's violins without Antonio." And because the master violin maker understood this, he said to himself, "If my hand slacked, I should rob God, since God cannot make a Stradivari violin without Antonio."[70] And He can't make a believing heart unless I choose to believe. William James put it well:

"The very [meaning] of [the] invisible world may . . . depend on the personal response [we] make to the religious appeal. . . . If this life be not a real fight, in which something is eternally gained for the universe by success, it is no better than a game of private theatricals from which one may withdraw at will. But it *feels* like a real fight—as if there were something really wild in the universe which *we* are needed to [help] redeem; and first of all to redeem our own hearts from atheisms and fears. For such a half-wild, half-saved universe our nature is adapted. The deepest thing in our nature is this . . . dumb region of the heart in which we dwell alone with our willingnesses and unwillingnesses, our faiths and fears."[71]

The Lord thus asks us to "be believing"—but for reasons intended to encourage our absolutely essential participation, He won't make the case for belief irresistible. He can't control whether we voluntarily choose to believe Him, to receive Him, to seek after Him. He can only offer us His hand, and if we elect to take it, *then* He can guide us toward whatever we uniquely need for own growth. He is so close, so available to those who have ears to hear and eyes to see. He is so close to those whose faith is not blind.

CHAPTER 11

A Witness More Powerful Than Sight

Not long ago a recently returned missionary asked us what it means that Apostles are "special witnesses of the name of Christ in all the world" (D&C 107:23) and that the Seventy are "especial witnesses . . . in all the world" (D&C 107:25). "Does that mean they have seen the Savior?" he asked reverently. I replied, "Well, it might mean that. But I also like what I once heard President Harold B. Lee say: 'I know by a witness more powerful than sight that Jesus is the Christ.'" Then we talked about the witness more powerful than sight. Here's a story about another young missionary who learned what that kind of witness is like.

First this little aside: In a rodeo, when a bronco rider is about to drop onto the quivering, flexing back of a snorting animal that is ready to rage and buck the instant a small chute is opened, a rodeo worker will probably shout to the rider, "Cowboy UP!" The rider then sits down hard, the chute springs open, the animal kicks and leaps around the arena, and the rider might well get bucked to kingdom come.

When we visited a mission in New Zealand, the mission president told us about an elder from Wyoming who had struggled mightily in his first few months. He was a tall, strong, and likable young man from a farm and ranch background. But interacting all day with total strangers in a foreign land had proven to be harder than he had ever imagined—and harder than he felt able to do. After repeatedly trying to face his daily labors, he finally told the mission president he just couldn't do missionary work and needed to go home.

The mission president counseled him for weeks with love, understanding, and encouragement. Then one day the elder showed up at the mission home with his companion—and with his bags packed. After one last interview, the president called the missionary's stake president, arranged for a plane ticket, then called his parents. When his father was on the line, the president said, "Your son needs to speak with you."

The president stayed as the father and son talked. In essence, the conversation was, "Dad, I'm so, so sorry! I know how much my mission matters to you, to me, to our whole family. But I can't do this. I just can't." The missionary listened tearfully for a few moments as his father spoke lovingly. But then the missionary's eyes bulged out in a look of total surprise. He moved the phone from his ear, looked at it briefly, and then hung it up, a look of shock on his face.

"What did he say, Elder?" asked the mission president. "He didn't hang up on you, did he?"

"No."

"Well, what did he say to you?"

"He said, 'Cowboy UP!'"

"Cowboy up? What in the world does THAT mean?"

The elder look at the floor thoughtfully. "It means I'm stayin'."

Soon after hearing this story, we met the missionary, who was then nearing the end of his mission. He had worked very hard and grown until he now set a superb example of both dedication and skill for the other missionaries as a mature person with both spiritual and intellectual depth. We asked him if the "cowboy up" story were true. He smiled sheepishly and said, "Yeah, it's true."

What did this young man now understand and embody that he didn't know, couldn't have understood, all those months earlier when he wanted to go home? By staying, serving, and stretching, he gradually discovered his own version of the witness more powerful than sight. Like the handcart pioneers, he came to know God in his extremities. He learned what it's like to move from innocent simplicity through demanding complexity to "other side" simplicity. We could see in his face that he had been tempered and proven.

The witness more powerful than sight applies especially to the role of actual, demanding experience in developing a witness that one knows the Savior. It is one thing to know *about* Him or even to see Him—but quite another to *know* Him. And that higher degree of "knowing" usually comes *after* complexity. Often it comes *because of* the complexity. The life story of the Apostle Paul vividly illustrates what this means.

When Paul was helping to persecute the early Christians, he was traveling on the road to Damascus when "suddenly there shined round about him a light from heaven: And he fell to the earth, and heard a voice saying unto him, Saul, Saul, why persecutest thou me? And he said, Who art thou, Lord? And the Lord said, I am Jesus whom thou persecutest" (Acts 9:3–5).

Paul saw Christ, or at least he saw the light in which Christ stood; and Paul heard His voice—he conversed one-on-one, aloud, with Him. But did Paul "know" Him because he saw and heard Him so directly? To the contrary, he asked, "Who art thou, Lord?" Then Paul, "trembling and astonished," asked, "what wilt thou have me to do?" (Acts 9:6).

As Paul staggered to his feet, he found that he'd been struck with a blindness that would last three days. But the Lord told him how to find Ananias, who would heal him. This was the beginning of Paul's journey of faith, but he needed to become blind in order to see. Not that one must see to believe, but one must believe in order to see. This was also just the beginning of Paul's encounter with complexity, for the Lord would now show Paul "how great things he must suffer for my name's sake" (Acts 9:16).

Paul was then baptized and willingly, even earnestly, began the missionary labors that would consume him for the rest of his life. The Lord therefore watched over him from the moment he began to preach Christ and Him crucified: "Saul increased the more in strength" (Acts 9:22). But in the years that followed, Paul would suffer, again and again, what he came to call "the afflictions of the gospel" (2 Timothy 1:8). On multiple occasions he was ship-wrecked, imprisoned, and persecuted as he labored to build tiny, struggling branches of the Church all over the Mediterranean.

As these forms of complexity increased, Paul eventually came to "glory in tribulations" (Romans 5:3). He learned from his own endless exertion in the Lord's cause that we can become "joint-heirs with Christ; if so be that we suffer with him" (Romans 8:17). Paul suffered for Him, with Him, doing His work, sacrificing for his missionary companions and the early Saints, continually af-flicted in their afflictions.

And he wasn't grumpy about a life of so much toil. Rather, his trials and his empathy for the travails of his fellow Saints softened his heart with the mellow affection that good missionaries often feel toward Church members: "We were gentle among you, even as a nurse cherisheth her children: So being affectionately desirous of you, we were willing to have imparted unto you, not the gospel of God only, but also our own souls, because ye were dear unto us" (1 Thessalonians 2:7–8).

After years of living through this relentless yet somehow glo-rious ordeal, Paul came to Mars Hill in Athens—a gathering place that sounds like the original and ancient version of Facebook: "For all the Athenians and strangers which were there spent their time in nothing else, but either to tell, or to hear some new thing" (Acts 17:21).

As Paul then spoke in this ancient center of democracy and philosophy to these lovers of debate for its own sake, he told them he had just passed by a monument they had built to celebrate that God is unknowable—and now he wanted to give them his personal, hard-won witness of Christ, for he now "knew" the unknown God: "Ye men of Athens," I saw the altar you have built "with this inscription, TO THE UNKNOWN GOD. *Whom therefore ye ignorantly worship, him declare I unto you*" (Acts 17:22–23; emphasis added).

Paul then said that the true God of heaven and earth had "made the world and all things therein," adding that if men and women will "seek the Lord . . . they might feel after him," for He is "not far from every one of us." Indeed, as some Greek poets have said, "we are also his offspring" (Acts 17:24, 27–28).

How could Paul "know" God this well now, in a way he simply didn't and couldn't have known Him when he saw and heard that stunning vision years earlier on the road to Damascus? He answered that question when he spoke of "Jesus my Lord: *for whom I have suffered the loss of all things . . . that I may know him, and . . . the fellowship of his sufferings*" (Philippians 3:8, 10; emphasis added).

Like the handcart survivors, Paul came to know God in his extremities, paying a price so high that at times it may have felt more like a burden than a privilege. Paul learned to know Him intimately through a lifetime of living in "the fellowship of his sufferings." For "how knoweth a man the master whom he has not served, . . . and is far from the thoughts and intents of his heart?" (Mosiah 5:13). Paul knew his Master because of what he learned from giving his heart and his life to Him. It was the witness more powerful than sight.

Joseph Smith's life story reveals a similar path. Joseph's original purpose in going to the grove was his anxious personal desire for his own forgiveness and salvation. The contention he sensed among the religious denominations in Palmyra distressed him primarily because of its effect on his personal quest, not because at age fourteen he was caught up in any macro-level worries about the historical state of Christianity: "The corruption and confusion in the churches seemed to stand in the way of his own salvation."[72] Thus when he later wrote about his vision, he at first "explained [it] as he must have first understood it, as a personal conversion. . . . It was the message of forgiveness and redemption he had wanted to hear."[73] And "in the years after his First Vision, Joseph . . . said little about his spiritual development. He had no sense of mission, no emerging prophetic identity."[74]

His concern for his personal standing with the Lord was also what motivated his crucial 1823 prayer—the one that was answered by Moroni's appearance in Joseph's bedroom. But Moroni's astonishingly specific message carried much larger implications— that "God had a work for me to do; and that my name should be had for good and evil among all nations."[75] Even though this message "wrenched Joseph" away from thinking only about his personal conversion,[76] it wasn't until he was writing his later accounts of the First Vision in 1835 and 1838 that he understood enough that his description of the vision shifted fully from his "own salvation" to "the opening of a new era of [religious] history."[77]

This natural development of Joseph's own understanding of who he was—and who God thought he was—illustrates the organic way Joseph needed to grow by actual experience in his understanding of what his having seen God really meant.

Like Paul, Joseph Smith came to know God best in his

extremities—as shown by many harrowing yet spiritually exquisite experiences. A few months after the Church was organized in 1830, for example, Joseph and Oliver Cowdery endured multiple personal attacks and legal challenges in the region between Harmony, Pennsylvania, and Colesville, New York. While fleeing from a mob, they were forced to run all night through a wooded and muddy area. At one point "Oliver was exhausted and Joseph almost carried him through mud and water." Near daybreak, a totally spent Oliver cried out, "How long Brother Joseph have we got to endure this thing?" Yet "at that very time Peter, James & John came to them" to restore the Melchizedek Priesthood and "ordained them to the Apostleship."[78]

In 1832 Joseph was in Kirtland, feeling pulled and torn trying to lead the Lord's people in faraway Missouri as well as in Ohio. After being mercilessly tarred and feathered, he fled from Kirtland to Missouri, only to find there that some of his most trusted followers were bickering and challenging him. On his return trip to Kirtland, Joseph's companion Newel K. Whitney broke his leg in a runaway stage accident. Joseph sent Sidney Rigdon on to Ohio, stayed to help Newel recover, and was himself afflicted with an intense bout of food poisoning that grounded him for a month. He finally reached Kirtland only to find trouble there with Sidney Rigdon, his counselor in the First Presidency. Joseph called it a season of "affliction and great tribulation."[79]

Yet even during this same hard season, Joseph received sections 76, 84, 88, and 93 of the Doctrine and Covenants—four of the most profound doctrinal revelations of the Restoration, all dealing with the theme of exaltation. This heavenly outpouring included his vision of the celestial kingdom and the three degrees of glory, along with doctrines about the greater and lesser priesthoods and receiving the "powers of godliness" in temples, four years before dedicating the Kirtland Temple. Somehow, rather than adversity blocking his access to the heavenly realm, "the switch from rebuke to vision suggests the relief Joseph Smith found in the contemplation of eternity. When the strains of managing Zion became too great, visions restored his strength."[80]

Six years later, Joseph was in Liberty Jail, separated from the members of the Church for five months and feeling utterly despondent. His letters to the Saints capture his frustration and his pleading to God over the horrendous Missouri persecutions: "Yea, O Lord, how long shall [thy people] suffer these wrongs and unlawful oppressions [?] . . . Let thy hiding place no longer be covered . . . let thine anger be kindled against our enemies. . . . Remember thy suffering saints" (D&C 121:3–6).

The next several sentences of Joseph's long letter are not included in the Doctrine and Covenants, even though other excerpts from that letter comprise the text for sections 121 through 123. The letter's full text lets us see a gradual but complete change in Joseph's mood—after his despair exhausts him and before the revelatory language of section 121 continues. After venting his understandable fury in those first verses of section 121, he pauses. Then his letter describes having received "kind and consoling" letters from Emma and other friends. The letters "were to our souls as the gentle air is refreshing, but our joy was mingled with grief because of the suffering of the poor and much injured saints."

Our "eyes were a fountain of tears but those who have not been inclosed in the walls of a prison without cause . . . can have but a little idea how [sweet] the voice of a friend is. One token of friendship . . . awakens . . . every sympathetic feeling" from the past and "seizes the present with a vivacity of lightning." It "grasps after the future with the fierceness of a tiger" until "finally all enmity, malice, and hatred . . . be slain victims at the feet of hope, and when the heart is sufficiently contrite then the voice of inspiration steals along and whispers . . ."[81]—and then he writes into the letter exactly what the Lord spoke to him in that moment, now given to us as D&C 121:7: *"My son, peace be unto thy soul; thine adversity and thine afflictions shall be but a small moment"* (emphasis added). The Lord continues, "Know thou, my son, that all these things shall give thee experience, and shall be for thy good" (D&C 122:7).

In the early years of the Restoration, God called Joseph *"my servant"* (D&C 1:17; emphasis added). After Joseph matured through turbulent yet at times sublime years of experiences like those just mentioned, God called him and his associates not "servants" but *"my friends"* (D&C 88:62; emphasis added). Joseph probably knew then what the Lord had said elsewhere: "Henceforth I call you not servants; for the servant knoweth not what his lord doeth: but I have called you friends; for all things that I have heard of my Father I have made known unto you" (John 15:15).

Then Joseph took one more step into the intimacy of knowing Him fully, when in his great extremity at Liberty Jail the Lord called him *"my son"* (D&C 121:7; emphasis added). Gradually he had grown from servant to friend to son. Like Paul, Joseph paid the price to know the Lord most fully as he suffered with and for Him, entering into the fellowship of Christ's sufferings.

What did Joseph learn in the "prison temple" of Liberty Jail that he didn't know, couldn't have known, on that 1820 spring day in the grove? Line upon line, opposition after opposition, it was the witness borne of experience—the witness more powerful than sight.

CHAPTER 12

Climbing to Know God

The process of receiving a personal witness of the Lord is not reserved for prophets alone, or just for older people. Think of the young elder who came to know God in ways he never would have, had he not been willing to "cowboy up" and face his fears—his version of complexity. A young sister missionary also shared with us how her personal challenges have helped her to keep reaching for God:

"I have a deep testimony . . . but it was a long, hard road to get there. I've struggled especially with questions and doubts about gender roles [and] LGBT [issues]. I often still feel like I'm more on the side of complexity than simplicity. [And yet working toward] the simplicity on the other side of complexity has been *anchoring* for me. [The] Savior's love reaches far beyond any complexity, any doubt or darkness or fear.

"So even though I don't understand the answer to each of my questions and concerns . . . I still love God with my whole heart and I know He is real. It's taken me a very long while to be able to say these things, but *because of the great difficulty of my journey to get here, the beliefs I do have are so much more precious to me*."[82]

Her experience shows that when we are surrounded by complexities and fears, if we don't choose to give the Lord and His Church the benefit of the doubt—if we don't "cowboy up"—we probably won't walk far enough down the road of faith and sacrifice to discover the simplicity of peace within the love of God.

We know a young man, Zachary, who, at the end of his mission to Asia, described to us his climb out of the naïve assumptions of his youth into some mind-bending, faith-challenging questions he had never before encountered. The people he had been sent to teach know little of God, and even less of their being His children. He allowed us into the anxiety of his thoughts as he faced this quandary: "How could I teach with conviction about someone I didn't understand? Who is God, anyway? I mean, who is He *really*? And who am I to Him?

"I had never honestly asked myself these basic questions. And I wasn't sure I could *totally* believe what the prophets, like Alma, were saying in the scriptures; I could believe some, but not *all*." With fresh candor, Zachary continued, "I didn't dare voice my doubts about this. I was a missionary! I didn't want anyone to know what I was really thinking, and what I *wasn't* feeling. But I was tired of carrying my questions around. So I decided to give ground to my doubts—at least not hide them from myself—and put my questions on trial as if in a debate between Alma and Korihor."[83]

Zachary then described taking the side of Korihor to test his questions and doubts against Alma, as if to say, "Convince me, Alma, that all things really do testify of Christ. Like really, *all* things?" Alma answered this challenge by referencing the scriptures, the testimonies of the prophets, and the creation of the earth itself (see Alma 30:44). After seriously searching for a response, Zachary, like Korihor, found that he had no countering evidence—could give no rebuttal. He sat there stupefied.

Then the imaginary debate continued with Zachary taking the place of Alma, who, drawing on teachings of other prophets, turned to Korihor and asked, "I hope for resurrection and eternal life with my family. What do you hope for?" (see Moroni 7:41).

The silence of Korihor's answer created for Zachary what he called "one of the most powerful moments of my life. The Korihor in me was dumbfounded, leaving me to ask, 'What *do I* hope for?'"

Zachary related to us how the clarity of this process and this question helped narrow the distance between himself and God. His newfound closeness brought with it, over time, a desire to talk with his Heavenly Father more than even his earthly parents, whom he loves dearly. "I talk with God all the time now, no matter where I am, and I feel Him with me." The closeness of this relationship then allowed Zachary not only to teach with conviction on his mission but to live with conviction now that he's home.

As Zachary narrated his wrestle with himself, it was as if we were watching him turn his questions into rungs on a ladder—his version of Jacob's ladder. It was obvious by the strength in his voice and the calm confidence in his countenance that not only was he now climbing that ladder but he knew why—to know the only true and living God and His Son, Jesus Christ, They who had provided the ladder to give us a way Home.

Each of us has access to this ladder, but we have to decide for ourselves if we will make the climb. The questions we encounter can become rungs that give us solid footing or they can become holes we fall through; it depends on how we handle them.

Zachary handled his questions honestly, but without compromising his values or slackening his standards of behavior. Neither did he allow his questions to become a crisis. He used what he already knew to help him work through what he didn't yet know. In his words, he "chose conviction over fearful uncertainty."

The elder who "cowboyed up," the sister who chose to love God despite her questions, and Zachary each turned their challenges into deeper conviction. They each used their complexities to gain more clarity about who they are, about who God is, and about their relationship with Him.

CHAPTER 13

Life and My Life

A big-picture review of the Western world's intellectual history offers a helpful perspective on why and how faith is not blind. One of the college classes I found most stimulating to teach was a course in which we looked at our own lives against the backdrop of the main ideas and cultural currents of European and American history. That framework provides a large-scale but striking illustration of the spiritual growth process we've been discussing here—from early simplicity to bewildering complexity to mature simplicity.

Two successive forms of early simplicity—the medieval Church and then the European kings—dominated Western civilization during centuries of relative stability. Then the twentieth century raised some shattering complexities that still grip most of the modern world in a web of intellectual, moral, and spiritual confusion. What enlightened simplicity can follow that complexity?

First, visualize a sketch on a blackboard showing a small square inside a larger square. The large macro square is "life" and the smaller micro square is "my life." The idea here is that, for centuries, large historical forces defined the outer square, thus defining for people what "life" in general meant. That overarching meaning of life often controlled the meaning of each individual's life—"my life."

We know that is a huge generalization, but we're making a very general point. Throughout the European Middle Ages, the Christian church and later the kings in various countries defined life's purpose as they understood it. They exerted such a dominant influence that for most people, the church and the kings also defined the micro "my life" of individuals within the larger framework, usually depending on their class or status. Most people accepted their place within the larger whole, usually because they believed that the church's explanation (or, later, the king's explanation) was God's will.

For example, think of the pieces on a chessboard, which represent the main figures in and around an ancient feudal manor. The king, queen, bishop, knight, rook, and pawns all have their places, and they are allowed to move only so far and in certain directions, based on their prescribed roles. In general, this era was high in "order" but low in "personal freedom."

The Enlightenment of eighteenth-century Europe (the Age of Reason) began to change this pattern because science and reason gradually replaced the church and the kings as the sources that explained the meaning of "life" in the big outer box. These explanations were typically more secular, competing with religion for social and cultural influence. Over time, science and reason came to replace or at least to dominate the religious explanations for "life," but people generally still looked to the given larger box as a frame of reference for their own lives. This era was still fairly high in order, but personal freedom accelerated as a whole series of scientific and political revolutions gradually overthrew the rigid authority of kings and churches.

Then came the twentieth century, when the big "life" box began to tremble and, for many people, it began to fall apart. Several major ideas that anticipated this century appeared in the late 1800s in the writings of people like Nietzsche, Darwin, Freud, and Marx. And the events that followed shook the foundations of traditional explanations: World War I, the Russian Revolution, the Great Depression, World War II and the Holocaust, the Bomb, and Communism.

These events, at times seeming to take their cues from those late-nineteenth-century European writers, led to a growing breakdown in society's confidence in an orderly universe. They also led to a widespread loss of confidence in the meaning of "life" as prescribed by the larger box. So this era, which became an age of relativism, offered a lower level of order, but a higher level of personal freedom. In some ways, these changes eventually offered almost too much personal freedom, leaving many people searching for direction but unable to find it.

To illustrate what had happened, our class discussed some simple examples that showed the breakdown of traditional explanations for "life." As we looked at each example, we would erase a small portion of the larger square until, as the discussion progressed, the larger box was completely erased. That left the smaller "my life" box on the blackboard, but with no stable or even discernible cosmic frame of reference around it.

The musical play *Fiddler on the Roof*, for example, was set in a Russian Jewish village in 1905, not long before the Russian Revolution destroyed the traditional reign of the czars. As the show opens, Tevye the milkman sings confidently about "Tradition." "Because of our traditions," he says, "every one of us knows who he is, and what God expects him to do. . . . Without our traditions, our lives would be as shaky as . . . a fiddler on the roof!"

Only a few years earlier, the actual shakiness of Tevye's traditional assumptions had been broodingly foretold by the German philosopher Friederich Nietzsche, who was the first to declare that "God is dead." But when he uttered that dark phrase, Niezsche "meant not only the [death of the] God of the Judeo-Christian faith but the whole range of philosophic *absolutes*, from Plato down to his own day. Because all Western values had been linked to those ultimate eternal 'values,' they crashed to earth with 'God's death.'" Nietzsche was thus "one of the first thinkers to stress the *absurdity* of human existence: the inability of our reason to comprehend our surroundings—though we are born to try."[84]

Within the next several decades, shattered by two World Wars and the economic collapse of the Great Depression, Austrian psychiatrist Viktor Frankl could write from his crushing years in a Nazi concentration camp, "The traditions which buttressed [man's] behavior are now rapidly diminishing. No instinct tells him what he has to do, and no tradition tells him what he ought to do." Soon he will not know "what he wishes to do." More and more, he will be governed by "what other people wish him to do."[85]

The twentieth century thus ushered in the age of relativism—not only moral relativism but scientific, philosophical, and artistic relativism. For instance, Einstein's theory of relativity heavily influenced science, which by then played a major role in defining the larger box. How fast is a fly moving when it buzzes around inside a speeding airplane? The fly's speed is "relative" to its frame of reference—the speed of the airplane. Matter and motion can be measured only with reference to given points or systems in time and space. And frames of reference aren't fixed—they are "relative" to changing circumstances. So virtually everything is relative.

In our class, we also looked at some visual and audio examples that show how parts of twentieth-century art, music, and literature reflected the breakdown of traditional frameworks for order and meaning. The arts do reflect the society and the times in which they are created. And in this case, some artistic creations (obviously not all creations—but enough to make the point) vividly reflected a collapsing belief in natural, objective laws and principles.

In art history, for example, we compared the "realistic" natural landscapes and portraits of nineteenth-century paintings with the often-unrealistic figures, colors, and shapes of modern art by painters like Picasso. Picasso was no longer trying to capture nature or objective reality in his work; rather, he wanted to get inside the mind of some individual observer, where he could imagine that person's subjective or inner perception of reality.

Similarly, looking at music history, we compared the orderly, harmonious sounds of Bach, Mozart, and Beethoven with the deliberately atonal (sounds without harmony) music of Stravinsky or Schoenberg. The work of these artists was part of "a more general effort, manifest in many fields, to re-examine the structure of the modern world even at the risk of destroying all one's assumptions of how the world should look or be understood."[86]

In literature, we compared the realistic novels of nineteenth-century Europe, such as those by Dickens, Tolstoy, and Jane Austen, with the work of such existentialist twentieth-century writers as Sartre, Camus, and Kafka. Some existentialist dramas, especially in the mid 1900s, were called "the theatre of the absurd," depicting the limited ability of human reason to comprehend, let alone explain, our surrounding circumstances.

For instance, in Samuel Beckett's celebrated 1955 play *Waiting for Godot*, two men carry on what usually sounds like meaningless conversation as they keep waiting, expecting someone named Godot to arrive as promised—but he never comes. Because Beckett believed that life has only the meaning the individual gives it, waiting for what or who never comes was for him a fair representation of mortality. In 1990, a poll conducted by the British Royal National Theatre found *Godot* the most significant English language play of the twentieth century,[87] partly because of how Beckett captured and reflected our shattered age:

"*Godot* has the pressure of our nightmarish history behind it. [It presents] man, naked, helpless, waiting . . . intensely alone, talking and talking to avoid feeling the . . . hellish silence—how can we not think of those killing prisons called concentration camps? The [800 people] who found *Godot* the most significant play of our century [realized] that it hauntingly reveals the darkest shadows of our frightening age . . . of man's pitiful vulnerability and unexplainable cruelty."[88]

Such literary approaches do suggest that the large objective box called "life" has mostly faded away, and that the subjective "my life" is only what we personally make of it. That can be a confusing and unsettling idea to contemplate. But it is not necessarily mean-ingless, especially when interpreted by such twentieth-century writers as Viktor Frankl, who wrote with deliberate optimism that by being left completely free to define the "why" of our own lives, we are responsible for (and have the opportunity for) giving our lives the meaning we desire.

By the middle of the twentieth century, the momentum of the revolutions that overthrew so many forms of the established order (religious, moral, political, and aesthetic) had in many ways pushed the historical pendulum from excessive order across the entire spec-trum past meaningful personal freedom into sheer chaos. This mo-mentum was partly driven by mass movements that passionately sought more freedom and more personal meaning, rather than just living out whatever role or purpose for "my life" was prescribed by someone else's frame of reference for "life." But the pendulum of that cultural momentum has now probably swung too far, leaving many people stranded in a place of helpless fear and nihilism—the "viewpoint that traditional values and beliefs are unfounded and that existence is senseless and useless."[89]

Constructive modern writers like Frankl tried to show that the modern vacuum of meaning was an opportunity for each individ-ual to define his or her life in a meaningful way. But it's difficult, perhaps impossible, to infer general cosmic meaning from purely

personal preferences. One person's individual choice won't necessarily lead to the universal absolutes that might—or do—exist.
That's partly because everything depends on each individual's experience. For instance, if one is having a nice day, does that mean
there is a Creator?

So amid today's modern disorder, where is the simplicity on
the other side of the complexity? Now that the gospel of Jesus
Christ has been restored, our opportunity to grasp the full meaning of "life" in the large box is once more fully on the earth. Our
lives need no longer be as shaky as a fiddler on the roof. But does
the individual still have some responsibility to fulfill his or her own
quest for meaning within the "given" framework of the gospel? Or
should we, like feudal pawns in the Middle Ages, just wait for God
to impose His absolute truths upon us without our active searching, participating, and striving?

Unlike the church of the Middle Ages, the restored gospel places enormous value on the concepts of personal freedom,
agency, and growth. That's what the premortal war in heaven was
about. The gospel's universal truths thus teach us how to engage a
personal quest for freedom and meaning. That quest really can't be
fulfilled without our active, wholehearted striving: participating,
enduring, searching, and overcoming all forms of opposition, uncertainty, and affliction.

The Restoration didn't simply "restore" the fixed absolutes that
traditional, apostate Christianity had imposed. Rather, it restored
the true combination of order and liberty that Christ Himself had
taught, such as, "And ye shall know the truth, and the truth shall
make you free" (John 8:32). This understanding allows the necessary interaction between (1) the striving to understand and accept
the absolutes of "life" that the Lord gives us, and (2) the striving to
exert ourselves with all the initiative and sense of responsibility for
"my life" that Viktor Frankl described.

Indeed, that's what the restored gospel is all about—helping us find and develop the fullest personal meaning of our own lives. That is precisely why we seek the guidance, the framework, of the gospel's universally true principles. Joseph Smith said it best: "God himself, finding he was in the midst of spirits and glory, because he was more intelligent, saw proper to institute laws whereby the rest could have a privilege to advance like himself. The relationship we have with God places us in a situation to advance in knowledge . . . that [we] may be exalted with himself."[90]

From a Latter-day Saint perspective, then, the revolutions against religious and political oppression (such as the Protestant Reformation and the American Revolution) were essential steps that prepared us for the Restoration—because the core ideas of individual liberty and individual development are absolutely crucial, and the medieval church made little allowance for those ideas.[91] Yet the Church that Jesus Himself established during His earthly ministry not only allowed for them, it fully taught and fostered them.

Drawing on the model for dealing with uncertainty described in chapter 2, we can see Stage One's idealistic dogmatism in the rigid order and absolutes of the Middle Ages. And we can see Stage Two complexity in the revolutionary reactions of the twentieth century that led us to moral relativism. But rather than just returning to Stage One, we now need Stage Three, with a personal-growth-oriented mixture between the real and the ideal, liberty and order—the very combination the Restoration has brought to a free but untethered and chaotic world.

Does God want us to sense that our individual choices about the meaning of our personal lives matter? Or, if we accept His larger cosmic purposes, would He prefer that we never think about that question? Consider the clear simplicity of the Primary song "I Am a Child of God," followed by the first three articles of faith. As we encounter our own version of today's chaotic complexities, we'll see that these ideas are now part of the restored conceptual framework for "life"—the simplicity beyond the modern complexity.

The Primary song first tells us who we are—literal children of a literal Heavenly Father. With this premise, the first article of faith states, "We believe in God, the Eternal Father, and in His Son, Jesus Christ, and in the Holy Ghost." The second article of faith states our personal agency and responsibility for "my life": "We believe that men will be punished for their own sins, and not for Adam's transgression." And the third suggests how each individual can be in harmony with the cosmos through interaction between the universal order and our personal agency: "We believe that through the Atonement of Christ, all mankind may be saved, by obedience to the laws and ordinances of the Gospel." This simple but divinely given explanation about the meaning of "life" helps each of us individually understand the origin and meaning of "my life."

It is quite possible to leave the Church today not because one has discovered a truer and more satisfying conceptual framework for "life," or because one has found a better church or religion. Rather, some may leave because they are going "from" something—maybe specific concerns about the Church's history or its leaders—rather than going "to" something else. Indeed, they may still instinctively long for the Restoration's basic understanding of the universe—of life—in the broad sense.

When people abandon the Restoration's "big box" about life's meaning but have nothing better to go to, their small "my life" box can be left with no frame of reference, no fixed stars, no complete orientation to the cosmos. It's hard to define one's cosmic structure only in terms of what it isn't. Perhaps that is why their disillusionment can beget the cosmic loneliness that leads to agnosticism or atheism. One thinks of the Savior's question to His disciples after some of His followers left Him: "Will ye also go away?" And Peter's reply, "To whom shall we go? thou hast the words of eternal life" (John 6:67–68).

Or perhaps some who leave still long for, and even practice, some Church teachings or traditions as "cultural Mormons," because those traditions still give them reassuring points of reference. Some may leave the Church over personal issues that are later resolved. Then they have a change of heart and come back. Sometimes by then, after they have raised their children outside the Church, they discover that while their children agreed with their problems about the Church, their children won't accept the solutions they have found.

Whatever one's issues with the Church might be, Stage Three simplicity is an invitation to see those disappointments as part of Stage Two complexity, rather than as a force so gigantic that it replaces the Restoration's cosmic grandeur in Stage Three. The simplicity beyond complexity has at its core "the words of eternal life." Attaining those words of life is worth the struggle needed to rediscover and reembrace them. Remember, "I would give *my life*," said Holmes, "for the simplicity on the other side of complexity."

CHAPTER 14

The Benefit of the Doubt and Moving Beyond Complexity

The personal story of South Africa's Khumbulani Mdletshe illustrates how, when we confront serious, hard questions, we can keep growing from innocent simplicity through complexity to refined simplicity—and how, in that process, our choosing to trust the Lord by performing acts of sacrifice allows Him to open doors for us. That's what giving Him the benefit of the doubt looks like.

Khumbulani was born in 1964 "under the dark cloud of apartheid [then] hanging over South Africa."[92] At age sixteen, he met two missionaries, the first friendly white people he'd known. After taking their message seriously, he joined the Church, and by 1985 he was a missionary in London. One day a complete stranger asked Elder Mdletshe why he would represent a racist church that denied its priesthood to black men. That was the first time he'd ever heard such a thing. He listened in shocked disbelief when his companion then told him that, as he understood it, the Church had withheld the priesthood from black Africans until 1978 because they were marked by the curse of Cain—the idea that "blacks descended from the same lineage as the biblical Cain, who slew his brother Abel. Those who accepted this view believed that God's 'curse' on Cain was the mark of a dark skin."[93]

Stunned by this bolt of complexity, especially after his traumatic years of apartheid at home, there was no way he could in good conscience continue his mission. Planning to announce his departure, he met with his mission president, Ed Pinegar, who confirmed that, yes, black African men were once denied the priesthood. Then he added, and "no one knows the reasons" why. But what matters is that "right now all worthy men can be ordained." Khumbulani later wrote, "I trusted my mission president. He always treated me like his own son. I believed him. Somehow, the Spirit bade me to accept his explanation and stay on my mission." That moment was so "life changing" that it "sustained me for more than three decades."

That didn't mean his confusion disappeared. In fact, the anger and hurt would often return when for years afterward he would hear other Church members still give "fallacious explanations" for the priesthood restriction. From the time his simplicity first crashed into this complexity, Khumbulani was clear-eyed, honest, and realistic; yet he was also meek enough to trust the Lord and the Church. When he couldn't imagine why no one had told him earlier about the ban, he thought perhaps his Church leaders in South Africa had temporarily chosen not to say anything that could wrongly imply that the Church had ever sympathized with apartheid. And in retrospect, he was sincerely grateful that his first missionaries hadn't mentioned the issue, because he hadn't then been prepared to hear it and would have rejected their message.

Toward the end of his mission, Khumbulani's attitude was rewarded by an inspired conversation with Wayne Shute, a BYU professor who was visiting London. When the mission president told him about the young elder's gifts and potential, Brother Shute helped arrange for Khumbulani to enroll at BYU–Hawaii. The Lord was opening another door. He earned a bachelor's degree at BYU–H and later a master's degree at BYU–Provo. He also endured in both places the continued frustration of hearing some people say in Church classes that the scriptures taught that Africans carried a curse.

Then he faced another moment of sacrifice. He had developed some close personal ties that pulled at him to stay in the United States. But he sensed, especially from his patriarchal blessing, that his family, the Lord, and the Church needed him in South Africa. So he left his friends and the comforts of Utah to return home to an uncertain future. Yet on his first Sunday in church back in South Africa, he met the woman he would later marry. His trust had led him to one more open door.

In his early years after returning home, Khumbulani at first struggled to find a job that matched his impressive qualifications from BYU. Then he found an excellent job as an NGO program evaluator in Johannesburg. This step led to further opportunities to help influence African education during a significant time of post-apartheid social reconstruction. But even with that much promise and stability in his life, as time went on the "we don't know why" answer from his mission president and a few other senior Church leaders wasn't enough to overcome his questions about the priesthood ban. He was troubled that the origins of the policy in Church history were so unclear. And he couldn't help wondering how much the Church's nineteenth-century leaders had been influenced by racist attitudes that grew out of the slavery era in American culture—even though he had learned enough about U.S. and Church history to see that the Church hadn't supported slavery, racism, and inequality as understood and practiced by many other American Christians.

While Khumbulani was still trying to resolve such questions, he was approached about leaving his employment to work for the Church Educational System in South Africa. At first he resisted that idea, until his wife suggested that they earnestly seek the Lord's direction. Then a prayerful visit to the temple reminded them that their "talents and skills have been given to us to assist in building the kingdom of God." So "without hesitation, we accepted the offer to join Church employment," which over time "proved to be the best decision we have ever made." Once more he had given the Lord the benefit of the doubt, not just as a mental exercise, but in choosing to sacrifice his promising secular career and to walk trustingly into another uncertain future. Only later would he realize that an even more promising door had thus been opened.

As time went on, other Church members repeatedly asked Khumbulani many of the same questions he himself still had about the priesthood ban and why a revelation was needed to remove it. His answers illustrate how, when we choose to give the Lord the benefit of the doubt, our righteous desires will help us find, understand, and teach a *plausible* pattern that supports some divine instruction—knowing that we can almost never "prove" conclusively that the pattern has a divine source. That was exactly what his mission president had done for him: "In my hour of need [he] could give me a *reason to believe* when no clear answers were readily apparent."

Speaking of the 1978 revelation, for example, Khumbulani told his children and his LDS institute students that "a revelation was needed to enlighten Church members . . . and to assist Church leaders who needed a doctrinal tool to teach those who would question . . . the change in policy." Moreover, "the revelation was needed as the Church matured in order that it might reach out to all people of the world." Khumbulani thus "learned to move forward despite my struggles with the history of restrictions on blacks in the Church."

Then once more his faith was rewarded. As a newly called Area Seventy from Africa, he attended a meeting for all of the Seventy and other general Church leaders just before a general conference in Utah. After President Thomas S. Monson had talked to the group and was leaving the room, President Monson paused, then spontaneously approached the three African Area Seventies who were seated together. He whispered to them, "Brethren, I would like to tell you that I worked with the man who gave the priesthood to all men." And something about that inspired moment with the Lord's prophet communicated beyond his words a spirit of peace that Khumbulani said allowed him and his two brethren to become "even stronger witnesses of the coming forth of Official Declaration 2. Any concerns or questions that any one of us might have had regarding race and the priesthood were no longer relevant. They were now resolved."

Khumbulani Mdletshe's personal story reflects both the process and the fruits of exercising a faith that is not blind—choosing to trust the Lord amid real complexities, showing trust by acts of real sacrifice, and seeing Him open real doors that He couldn't open, even for our benefit, if we didn't offer Him our trust. Khumbulani's attitude is like Richard Bushman's. Even with Richard's nearly incomparable skills for research and analysis on Church history issues, he has encountered his share of unanswerable puzzles. When that happens, he has said, "I just ask myself, 'What can this teach me about God?'"

Khumbulani's story illustrates American writer Peter Wehner's recent description of why faith can be better than doubt, and better than demanding proof before acting:

"Faith is prized within the Christian tradition [because] it involves trust that would not be needed if the existence of God were subject to a mathematical proof. What God is seeking is not our intellectual assent so much as a relationship with us. . . . Faith is a greater blessing than proof because it gives us a relationship with Jesus. All good relationships are bound together by love. And love is always an expression of faith. . . . We are changed by what we love more than [by] what we think."[94]

Khumbulani's confidence in his mission president reinforced his faithful instincts enough that he gave the Church the benefit of the doubt, and he sacrificed by staying. When the "we don't know why" answer became less satisfying and he felt enticed to stay in the United States, the closeness of his relationship with the Lord took priority, and he returned to South Africa. When he wondered about his employment, his temple covenants prompted him to walk again beyond the edge of the light. Gradually the tension of his complexities diminished as he felt the calm trust of refined, "other-side" simplicity. Nourished by his love for the Lord and the Lord's love for him, he was changed more by that love than by his thinking.

CHAPTER 15

The Spirit of the Army

God has always interacted with His children through the cru-cible of mortal complexities. In that crucible, it is always ours to decide whether we trust Him.

When President Wilford Woodruff announced the Manifesto in 1890, he said, "The Lord will never permit me or any other man who stands as President of this Church to lead you astray" (Official Declaration 1). Yet President Russell M. Nelson has also asked us to "Give your leaders a little leeway to make mistakes," because, as President Dallin H. Oaks put it, "We don't believe in the infallibility of our leaders."[95]

Whatever else "won't lead you astray" means, it does not mean the Lord's prophet will always tell us exactly what to do. Sometimes he asks us to seek our own direction, part of helping us learn how to develop our trust in God. For example, speaking in 1890 of whether the Church should keep or abandon plural marriage when the U.S. government was about to confiscate the Church's temples, President Woodruff said the Lord had "told me to ask the Latter-day Saints a question;" namely, "which is the wisest course," to give up the temples or to give up plural marriage? And if they would listen and find their own answers, "by the Spirit and power of God, they would all answer alike." Then with no edicts, he concluded, "I leave this with you . . . to contemplate and consider" (Official Declaration 1).

In a moment of inspired insight, President Woodruff was calling upon the sacred power of each Church member's personal relationship with God to find for himself or herself the answer the prophet already knew. That insight can help teach us how we can in good conscience give the Lord and His Church the benefit of the doubt as we work through our complexities.

Prompted by Khumbulani Mdletshe's story, let us apply that idea to the topic of race and the priesthood. It is no small matter to conclude, as some Church members do today, that all of the First Presidencies from Brigham Young through Harold B. Lee were simply wrong in maintaining the priesthood and temple restriction for over a century—not just that some of their theories to explain the ban were mistaken (as the Church has acknowledged),[96] but that the ban itself was wrong.

There is a difference between the restriction and possible reasons for it. As President Oaks said, "I decided a long time ago that I had faith in the command and I had no faith in the reasons that had been suggested for it."[97] Further, he added, "In general, the Lord rarely gives reasons for the commandments and directions He gives to His servants."[98]

This issue matters. Concluding that the priesthood restriction itself was wrong makes it more likely that we would hold back from giving the Lord and His prophets the benefit of the doubt about other important questions.

Recent survey data found that "nearly two-thirds of self-identified Latter-day Saints say they either know or believe" that this restriction was God's will for the Church until 1978.[99] Still, we hear two contradictory narratives these days among active Church members.

First, some say that our nineteenth-century Church leaders' views about black Africans simply reflected the racist attitudes of that era's larger American culture. But, they say, historical context should not be relevant to eternal truth. And with the hindsight of today's more egalitarian time, it is clear that the priesthood and temple restriction was simply wrong. Our leaders should have been more in tune with God and more courageous. In addition, a few black men did receive the priesthood during Joseph Smith's time.

Second, others say that the restriction itself was not a mistake. We shouldn't interpret nineteenth-century racial history through the lens of twenty-first-century assumptions about what our Church leaders could and should have understood and done that long ago in the name of fairness and equality. They say the Lord had His own reasons for the ban. Anciently, access to the gospel was limited for centuries, until the revelation to Peter about Cornelius. And the 1978 revelation was all part of His plan in the long historical sequence of taking the gospel message to "every people." Only He could judge when those people, the Church, and society were ready for this culminating step.

In searching for some reconciliation between these viewpoints, we once made the effort to review the plausible historical evidence supporting each view. The evidence does matter, because even though rational argument and evidence do not by themselves create belief, such evidence does "maintain a climate in which belief may flourish."[100] Historical evidence alone is not always capable of totally proving or disproving scriptural and prophetic claims, but it does help those who want to give the benefit of the doubt to the Lord's prophets to know that there is at least a rational basis that supports their choice. Call it "informed faith."

But then we paused, sensing that where we place the benefit of the doubt in resolving such complexities finally turns on larger questions than just how plausible the evidence is. Especially with sensitive and complex subjects, it's easy to get bogged down in details and differences of opinion about "evidence" that divert attention from the ultimate and very personal process of deciding how, where, and to whom we should give the benefit of the doubt in close cases.

As one friend said, "Not all uncertainties need to be resolved intellectually. Blind faith is simple, easy, and ultimately dangerous, but the benefit of the doubt is something earned by thought and experience that is then lovingly, charitably given to others, not because you have to," or because of plausible evidence, "but because you love and trust" the Brethren—just as God extends "the arm of mercy towards them that put their trust in him" (Mosiah 29:20), "giving each one of us the benefit of what surely must be some well-founded doubt" about our ultimate worthiness.[101]

Also regarding how to resolve unsettled questions after we've gathered all of the available evidence, recall Moroni's promise about how to learn whether the Book of Mormon is true. Before applying the familiar test in Moroni 10:4–5, or before deciding where to place the benefit of the doubt, Moroni's prior first step is, "I would exhort you that when ye shall read these things . . . that ye would remember how merciful the Lord hath been unto the children of men, from . . . Adam [until now] . . . , and ponder it in your hearts" (Moroni 10:3).

Why begin our quest with such remembering and pondering? Because gratitude turns our hearts to God, and because He "has an infinitely long track record of lovingly pointing us in the right direction." Then our basic *attitude* looks beyond the current culture and the historical evidence to the higher "vantage point of a loving God who has always worked patiently through flawed people to accomplish a perfect mission."[102]

That attitude toward trusting God need not be complicated. One friend experienced it this way. As a child he was perplexed in wondering what "eternal life" could possibly mean—"the prospect of living forever seemed impossibly boring to me. I could barely sit through three hours of church. [So I] took my concern to God with all the sincerity of a young boy and got a powerful answer:

'Trust me. It'll be good.'" Ever since, he has wanted eternal life, not because he fully understands it, but because "God spoke to me and I trust Him."[103]

The presence of a plausible explanation for whatever complex issue we're wrestling with can be reassuring and inform our faith. Yet our choices to believe can't—and therefore shouldn't—always count on complete rational support. Choosing to calm the chaos of our uncertainties by extending to the Lord and His Church the benefit of the doubt preserves our capacity to make the sacrifices, large and small, that our consecration requires—from accepting mission calls and paying tithing to accepting other Church callings, fasting, and wearing the temple garment with respect.

We take some guidance here from what President Spencer W. Kimball said about Peter denying Christ three times.[104] Perhaps the standard interpretation is correct—Peter denied knowing Christ because he was human, weak, and afraid. On the other hand, said President Kimball, it is possible that the Savior's statement was not a prediction but a request for Peter to deny knowing Him in order to ensure Peter's future leadership for the Church. Which interpretation is correct? Like Wilford Woodruff, Spencer Kimball left that for us to decide.

So it is with the priesthood restriction—or with any official Church position. Perhaps the Brethren made a mistake. But perhaps not. Was it a mistake for Peter to withhold the gospel from the Gentile world until the revelation described in Acts 10? Did the Lord give Peter the reasons for that revelation? Would the Lord give His prophet instructions without also giving reasons for the instruction? He might, partly because we may not yet be able to understand His reasons. Think of the Lord's asking Mormon to include the small plates of Nephi, asking Adam and Eve to offer sacrifices, and the annunciation to Mary. In each case, He didn't initially give them reasons for what He asked them to do.

We can't "prove" enough about such questions to answer them with certainty. So the Lord wants us to choose where to repose our trust, through a demanding, searching, personal process that connects us to Him. He wants us to consider what all of our experience teaches us about whether we can trust Him.

Earlier chapters explored why the Lord so often puts us in such places, where we're not forced by the circumstances to believe, even as He then invites us to "be believing." For "as many as *received* him, to them gave he power to become the sons of God, even to them that [choose to] believe on his name" (John 1:5, 12; emphasis added). Why? Because something happens to people who choose to receive Him. They learn. Following His will changes them. Our uncoerced choices set in motion the process of becoming like Him.

The Lord sees an infinitely bigger picture than we do. If we want the blessing of that infinite perspective, we give Him and His prophet the benefit of the doubt—which is ultimately a trust issue. And only if we extend our trust is He able to help us learn what He wants us to learn. We do value what we *discover* far more than we value what we're *told*.

Paying too much attention to "evidence" can cause us to base our trust entirely on reason, or on an expectation of certain blessings. That isn't trust so much as it is bargaining. Unless we give Him our "noncontingent trust" (trust that doesn't depend on a particular outcome), He can't lead us where He knows we need to go—a destination often unknown to us.

On the other hand, what does "contingent trust" look like? We have mentioned the returned missionary who said he had left the Church because "the Church just didn't meet my expectations." His expectations—his personal view of what was best for himself— defined what he would allow the Lord to ask of him or do for him. His trust was contingent.

So what does *non*contingent trust look like? Consider some

examples. Nathan Leonhardt, a BYU student, told us how he has moved through the three stages of dealing with uncertainty. He said he's learned about "the paradox that Christ's Atonement has the power to bridge the gap between the real and the ideal, yet it often doesn't." He has known his share of disappointed expectations, learning what it's like "to put complete faith in a righteous desire, plead for assistance, and still not see the gap bridged." He wouldn't have had "the strength to reconcile this paradox with my previously closed eyes/open heart worldview. In reconciling this paradox, I take comfort in the examples of devoted disciples who have taught me to have faith in Christ, noncontingent on the outcome."

Nathan continued: "For every Shadrach, Meshach, and Abednego who are saved from the flames (Daniel 3), an Abinadi is allowed to burn (Mosiah 17). For every wayward Alma the Younger that is brought to the light from a pleading, faithful parent (Mosiah 27), a Laman and Lemuel continue to stray (1 Nephi). For every 2,000 stripling warriors who leave the battle with nothing more than wounds (Alma 56:56), 1,005 are left to be slain by the sword (Alma 24:22). For every Ammon who brings thousands of souls to repentance (Alma 26:22), a Mormon and Moroni labor all the days of their life and never see the fruits of their labor (Moroni 9:6). For every blind to see, deaf to hear, and lame to walk (Matthew 11:5), the experience of unfathomable suffering awaits in Gethsemane (Matthew 26). *However* . . .

"For every Abinadi who is burned, sometimes an Alma takes the doctrine to heart and begins a lifetime in service to God (Mosiah 17). For every 1,005 who are left to be slain, sometimes we see 'the Lord worketh in many ways to the salvation of his people' as more souls are brought to repentance than the number who perished (Alma 24:27). For every 'thy will be done' in submission to the agony of Gethsemane (see Matthew 26:39), there is a prayer too beautiful to be recorded, the blessing of children one by one, angels descending from the opened heavens, and tears streaming down the face from One who can finally declare full joy (3 Nephi 17)."[105]

When our faith is based on trust and not on certain expected blessings, we can endure any trial.[106] We don't know if, when, or how He will deliver us in the short term, but when we meekly yield to Him our noncontingent trust, He will always deliver us in the long term.

Job personifies noncontingent trust. Satan taunts God by saying Job's trust is contingent: "Thou hast blessed the work of his hands, and his substance is increased in the land. But put forth thine hand now, and [take away] all that he hath, and he will curse thee to thy face" (Job 1:10–11). In other words, Job appears to be faithful, but he lives that way only because it makes him prosper. So God lets Satan have his way with Job. A string of horrific traumas strikes Job, his family, his servants, and his property. But Job then falls to the ground and worships, saying, "the Lord gave, and the Lord hath taken away; blessed be the name of the Lord" (Job 1:20–21). Satan misread Job. But the Lord knew his heart, his noncontingent trust.

In our own day, here is where Richard Bushman's noncontingent trust has taken him—and where ours can take us:

"I know the arguments against the [Book of Mormon's] historicity, but I can't help feeling that the words are true and the events happened. I believe it in the face of many questions. . . . Unanswerable as some questions are, we need not lament the questions they bring. The strain of believing in unbelieving times is not a handicap or a burden. It is a stimulus and a prod. . . . And . . . we are in this together."[107]

Since we are in fact in this together, what happens when we let the particular become the general, and we imagine an entire host of people whose faith is noncontingent—based on trust and not on bargained-for blessings? That image would tell us what Wilford Woodruff might have meant when, instead of giving the Saints "the answer" about the rightness or wrongness of the Manifesto, he gently asked them to find their own answer "by the Spirit and power of God." And if they would, he said, "they would all answer alike . . . and believe alike." How could he know they would?

Because that is "the spirit of the army."

In an unforgettable section of *War and Peace*, Leo Tolstoy narrates Napoleon's irresistible advances deep into Russian territory. Then comes a furious struggle not far from Moscow, the Battle of Borodino, when the Russian army holds the French army to what looks at best like a bloody draw. What happens next is the turning point of the great 1812 war, shifting the momentum to favor the Russians.

When the Russian commander, Kutuzov, is deciding whether to launch a new attack immediately after Borodino, Tolstoy writes that when the old general listened to the reports from the field, he seemed "not interested in the words being spoken, but rather in something else—in the expression of face and tone of voice of those who were reporting." By long experience, Kutuzov knew that battles are not decided as much by logistical details about positions and cannons, "but by that intangible force called the spirit of the army."

Both armies had lost thousands of men at Borodino. Kutuzov's advisers pressed him to retreat, as they'd always done against Napoleon. But Kutuzov sensed that his men knew their backs were against the symbolic wall of Moscow, and he had felt them rally in some profound inner way. So he stunned his strategists by ordering an attack the next day: "[The French] are repulsed everywhere, for which I thank God and our brave army! . . . and tomorrow we shall drive him from the sacred soil of Russia." And Kutuzov sobbed.

Then, writes Tolstoy, "by means of that mysterious indefinable bond . . . known as 'the spirit of the army,'" Kutuzov's battle order spread "from one end of the army to the other." And even though the details were somewhat garbled, "the *sense* of his words spread everywhere," because his message "was *not the outcome of cunning calculations, but of a feeling that lay in [his] soul as [it did in the soul] of every other Russian.*" And his exhausted men "felt comforted and inspirited."[108]

Tolstoy's theory of history was that we "must leave aside kings, ministers, and generals, and study the . . . small elements by which the masses are moved."[109] He believed it was not superior strategy or charismatic leadership but the all-pervading "simplicity, goodness, and truth" of the Russian people and their army—even amid their weaknesses—that "defeated a power that did not respect simplicity and that acted out of evil and falseness."[110]

Some years ago, a thoughtful non-LDS professor of family law from Japan visited the BYU campus for a week, living in a guest room in a student dorm. Each day he ate with, talked with, and watched BYU students and faculty. When he was leaving for home, he said to me, "I have never seen such a place. This campus is an island of hope in the land of the Apocalypse. I must know the mystery behind all the shining eyes." I replied that the mystery behind the students' shining eyes is "the spirit of the army" of the Saints, a spirit of "simplicity, goodness, and truth" that animates the BYU community and every ward and branch of the Church.

Those who criticize the Latter-day Saints for blindly following their leaders don't really understand the origin and meaning of this spirit. They seem unable to grasp that those shining eyes are not "the outcome of cunning calculations" but are the fruits of intensely personal convictions developed through thousands of private stories and struggles.

President Wilford Woodruff and President Russell M. Nelson know all about those private struggles and stories. They've seen them in their own lives and in ours. President Gordon B. Hinckley was perhaps thinking of such stories when someone asked him, "If you do not use the cross, what is the symbol of your religion?" He replied, "the lives of our people." Our Church members' lives are "the most meaningful expression of our faith and, in fact, therefore, the symbol of our worship. It is that simple, my brethren and sisters, and that profound, and we'd better never forget it."[111]

So, for us, what is the spirit of the army? Along with the great scriptural and prophetic witnesses of Christ, President Hinckley added "the witness of millions who, by the power of the Holy Spirit, . . . bear solemn testimony of His living reality. That testimony has been their comfort and their strength."[112] We pray often for the prophet and his Brethren. Consider what it means that they also pray often for us. We're all part of the same army, each with an individually sought and heavenly bestowed testimony within our souls.

Today, when our backs are against the wall of a degraded, secular society whose acid eats at the roots of our children's faith, or our own, do we just look to our prophet-leader to fix it, or do we also look into our own souls? When we speak of giving the Lord and His Church the benefit of the doubt, what or who is "His Church"? We are giving our trust not only to the Lord and His prophet. We give it also to the gospel and its power—the combined personal assurances from all the Latter-day Saints that the Lord keeps His promises. In all their paradoxes and uncertainties, they reflect those assurances in the shining eyes of a million personal discoveries.

And, as one young mother said, the biggest reason to give the Church the benefit of the doubt is that it has the Lord's priesthood power. So as we extend trust, that power stays with us: "Hold on thy way, and the priesthood shall remain with thee" (D&C 122:9).

Many in today's community of Saints feel great empathy and love for their family and friends who have unsettled religious feelings. The stalwarts in this community are not just active in the Church, they are consecrated disciples of Christ. They are fighting through their own uncertainties to resolve their questions in favor of the Lord and His Church. Many of them live in the simplicity beyond complexity, and they reach out to "lift up the hands which hang down, and strengthen the feeble knees" (D&C 81:5).

It will strengthen us if we can trust the hard-won personal testimonies from the thousands upon thousands who have read, thought about, and prayed over the Book of Mormon, year after year; who have served missions of faith and sacrifice all over the world; who have intimately felt the Lord's influence, His closeness to them; who have seen the promises of Christ's redemption bear sweet fruit in their lives and the lives of those closest to them; who have often told the Joseph Smith story to their children, their friends, and to strangers—and felt the spirit of its simple, pure truth. We "are compassed about with so great a cloud of witnesses" (Hebrews 12:1).

Who are the people in this army? These are they of the noncontingent trust, who have grown beyond complexity to the calm trust of informed simplicity; who trust prophetic leadership not as the outcome of cunning calculations, but because they have discovered the same convictions and feelings in their own souls. They have found their own answers, even if not yet all of the answers they seek. They know enough that they cast not away their confidence. They are not of them who draw back (see Hebrews 10:35–39).

Who are the people in this army? "Behold, the righteous, the saints of the Holy One of Israel, they who . . . have endured the crosses of the world, and despised the shame of it, they shall inherit the kingdom of God . . . and their joy shall be full forever" (2 Nephi 9:18).

"These are they which came out of great tribulation [and complexity], and have washed their robes . . . white in the blood of the Lamb" (Revelation 7:14).

"To him that *overcometh* will I grant to sit with me in my throne, even as I also overcame" (Revelation 3:21; emphasis added).

True faith is not blind, or deaf, or dumb. Rather, true faith *sees* and *overcomes* her adversary.

Descending to Ascend

When our living becomes rooted in our relationship with the Divine, the chaos and confusion that form the crossfire of complexity give way to a hush that is created for us by the Creator Himself. The promise of such peacefulness gives each of us hope to keep climbing our own Jacob's ladder. This climb is composed of all the day-by-day choices we have to make, all the sacrifices that are required for our sanctification.

Eventually, then, we come into the calm of spirit that is mature simplicity, and there we realize that another passage lies ahead, full of its own complexities. Stage Three is not our final destination. The simplicity that lies on the *far* side of Holmes's complexity is the simplicity that lies on the *front* side of another sanctifying passage.

If we are going where we say we want to go, we must be willing to submit to the pressures of this next passage. Can we stay sweet, meek, and merciful even in the crucible of others' taunting doubts and our own Gordian-like questions? Do we have the strength to follow Christ all the way through Gethsemane to Calvary while not becoming embittered along the way by the bitterness of whatever cup is ours to drink? As Elder Neal A. Maxwell said, "If we are serious about our discipleship, Jesus will eventually request each of us to do those very things which are most difficult for us to do."[113]

The seasoned simplicity of Stage Three takes us again to the temple ready to submit deeper still to the code of conduct our Master has stepped off for us in both His words and deeds. Our temple worship prior to entering Stage Three is, comparatively speaking, mere box checking and "I know not" kind of going through the motions. Blind obedience is a start—it was for Adam and Eve. But our now-informed faith prepares us—requires us—to choose whether we will proceed through the next passage, eyes and hearts wide open to its compression.

Such a space is completely outside the comfort zone of our natural man. But our trust in the promises of the Comforter—His rest, His unspeakable joy—makes the passage possible. And we trust that on the other side of this passage, this proverbial Rocky Ridge, we'll look back and agree that the price of passage was a privilege to pay.

In the early years of his life, our returned missionary friend Zachary has begun his own climb toward this sanctifying passage— the one in which our descent into the depths of our own souls is also our ascent into the holiness of heaven. In the later years of his life, President James E. Faust gave us a glimpse of his experience with this hallowing climb:

"In the Gethsemanes of life which we all have, and often in my present calling, I have gone to my knees with a humble spirit to the only place I could for help. I often went in agony of spirit, earnestly pleading with God to sustain me in the work I have come to appreciate more than life itself. I have, on occasion, felt a terrible aloneness of the wounds of the heart, of the sweet agony, the buffetings of Satan, and the encircling warm comfort of the Spirit of the Master.

"I have also felt the crushing burden, the self-doubts of inadequacy and unworthiness, the fleeting feeling of being forsaken, then of being reinforced an hundredfold. I have climbed a spiritual

Mount Sinai dozens of times, seeking to communicate and to receive instructions. It has been as though I have struggled up an almost real Mount of Transfiguration and, upon occasion, felt great strength and power in the presence of the Divine. A special, sacred feeling has been a sustaining influence and often a close companion."[114]

When in the depth of struggle to ascend my own Sinais, when the air is thin and cold and my energy spent, I have felt His strength—not always, but enough.

When our family encircled our baby grandson's tiny casket under that big, old tree at the cemetery, I felt His comfort with such surety that my belief in the Resurrection became spiritual knowledge that we would be with Devin again someday.

When, as a college freshman, I knelt penitent by my bed after some indiscretions, pleading for my inner vessel to be clean and clear, I felt His forgiveness lightening and reassuring.

While I was writing on the blackboard teaching the Relief Society sisters in my student ward, I felt His confirmation, in that instant, that the words coming out of my mouth were not mine but His.

When our oldest granddaughter knelt at the temple altar with her chosen companion, I felt hints of the eternal joy He promises—that if that starry-eyed young couple would work and forgive and play and rest with Him in their relationship, their sealing would be beautiful beyond time.

In such times, when my heart has broken open with tenderness for Him, there have been moments when He has allowed me to feel His tears falling with mine. My faith flows from such moments and assures me that with Him—because of Him—our barren wildernesses can be turned into watered gardens.

Notes

1. J. Spencer Fluhman, Kathleen Flake, and Jed Woodworth, eds., *To Be Learned Is Good: Essays on Faith and Scholarship in Honor of Richard Lyman Bushman* (Provo: Neal A. Maxwell Institute for Religious Scholarship, Brigham Young University, 2017), 295–306; emphasis added.
2. Fluhman, Flake, and Woodworth, eds., *To Be Learned Is Good*, 295–306.
3. John Milton, *Areopagitica* (1644).
4. Reid N. Nibley, unpublished poem, copy in our possession.
5. https://en.wikiquote.org/wiki/Talk:Oliver_Wendell_Holmes_Jr.
6. Gilbert K. Chesterton, *Orthodoxy* (Garden City, NY: Image Books, 1959), 69–70.
7. Chesterton, *Orthodoxy*, 71.
8. J.R.R. Tolkien, *The Fellowship of the Ring*, 2nd ed. (Boston: Houghton Mifflin, 1965), 182.
9. H. Donl Peterson, "Translation and Publication of the Book of Abraham," in *Encyclopedia of Mormonism* (New York: Macmillan, 1992), 134.
10. *Teachings of Presidents of the Church: Joseph Smith* (Salt Lake City: The Church of Jesus Christ of Latter-day Saints, 2007), 419.
11. Richard Lyman Bushman, *Joseph Smith: Rough Stone Rolling* (New York: Alfred A. Knopf, 2005), 133.
12. Neal A. Maxwell, *That Ye May Believe* (Salt Lake City: Deseret Book, 1992), 191–92.
13. T. S. Eliot, "Little Gidding," 5.26–29, in *Four Quartets* (London: The Folio Society, 1968), 55.
14. Wikipedia, "Betsy Ross," https://en.wikipedia.org/wiki/Betsy_Ross.
15. Neil Postman, *The Disappearance of Childhood* (New York: Vintage, 1994).
16. Leonard J. Arrington and Dean May, "A Different Mode of Life: Irrigation and Society in Nineteenth Century Utah," *Agricultural History*, Vol. 49, 1975.
17. David Ignatius, "How to Protect Against Fake Facts," *Washington Post*, November 23, 2017.
18. Email from Bud Scruggs to Bruce Hafen, July 12, 2107.
19. Ari Shapiro interview with David Zax, *All Things Considered*, National Public Radio (NPR), October 20, 2017.
20. Sam Levin, "Google and YouTube spread false claims Texas shooting suspect had leftwing ties," *The Guardian*, November 6, 2017, online edition.

Notes

21. E.g., Matt Apuzzo and Sharon LaFraniere, "13 Russians Indicted as Mueller Reveals Effort to Aid Trump Campaign," *New York Times,* February 16, 2018.

22. Laura Sydell, "Can You Believe It? On Twitter, False Stories Are Shared More Widely Than True Ones," *All Things Considered*, NPR, March 12, 2018, nhttps://www.npr.org/people/2101272/laura-sydell.

23. Jack Nicas, "Google Has Picked an Answer for You—Too Bad It's Often Wrong," *Wall Street Journal,* November 16, 2017.

24. Christie Aschwanden, "There's No Such Thing as 'Sound Science,'" fivethirtyeight.com/features/the-easiest-way-to-dismiss-good-science-demand-sound-science.

25. Aschwanden, "There's No Such Thing."

26. Eric d'Evegnee email to Bruce Hafen, December 6, 2017.

27. Letter from Joseph Smith to Daniel Rupp, June 5, 1844, http://www.josephsmithpapers.org/paper-summary/history-1838–1856-volume-f-1–1-may-1844–8-august-1844/1#full-transcript.

28. Ezra Taft Benson, "To the Mothers in Zion," fireside address delivered February 22, 1987, and later printed as a pamphlet. See "President Benson Lauds Blessings of Motherhood," *Ensign*, May 1987.

29. Benson, "To the Mothers," quoting David O. McKay, *Gospel Ideals* (Salt Lake City: Improvement Era, 1953), 452.

30. Gordon B. Hinckley, "Stay on the High Road," *Ensign*, May 2004.

31. "The Family: A Proclamation to the World," *Ensign*, November 2010, 129.

32. Summarized in *The Motherhood Study,* Institute for American Values, 2005, americanvalues.org/catalog/the motherhoodstudy.

33. See Joseph Chilton Pearce, *The Biology of Transcendence* (Rochester, VT: Park Street Press, 2002).

34. For further discussion of this theme, see Bruce C. Hafen and Marie K. Hafen, *The Contrite Spirit* (Salt Lake City: Deseret Book, 2015), chapter 13.

35. Letter from Joseph Smith to Daniel Rupp.

36. "'One Step Enough': Replacing Fear with Faith," BYU Devotional, June 30, 1992.

37. *Richard Douglas Poll Papers.* University of Utah Marriott Library Special Collections. Retrieved 2017–02–15.

38. Thomas F. O'Dea, *The Mormons* (Chicago, IL: University of Chicago Press, 1957), 240.

39. www.pewforum.org/2012/01/12/mormons-in-america-beliefs-and-practices.

40. Rod William Horton and Vincent Foster Hopper, *Backgrounds of European Literature* (New York: Appleton-Century, 1954), 248.

41. H.D.F. Kitto, *The Greeks* (Baltimore, MD: Penguin, 1969), 8.

42. Daniel C. Peterson, "Editor's Introduction: 'What Has Athens to Do with Jerusalem?' Apostasy and Restoration in the Big Picture," *F.A.R.M.S. Review of Books,* vol. 12, no. 2 (2000), xii.

43. Bruce C. Hafen, *A Disciple's Life: The Biography of Neal A. Maxwell* (Salt Lake City: Deseret Book, 2002), 380.

44. Hafen, *Disciple's Life,* 379.

45. Hafen, *Disciple's Life,* 12.

46. Hafen, *Disciple's Life,* 558–59.

Notes

47. http://www.josephsmithpapers.org/paper-summary/history-1838–1856-volume-b -1–1-september-1834–2-november-1838/177.

48. http://www.josephsmithpapers.org/paper-summary/history-1838–1856-volume-b -1–1-september-1834–2-november-1838/306.

49. http://www.josephsmithpapers.org/paper-summary/history-1838–1856-volume-b -1–1-september-1834–2-november-1838/180.

50. As quoted in James E. Faust, "The Refiner's Fire," *Ensign*, May 1979.

51. http://www.josephsmithpapers.org/paper-summary/history-1838–1856-volume-b -1–1-september-1834–2-november-1838/150.

52. http://www.josephsmithpapers.org/paper-summary/history-1838–1856-volume-b -1–1-september-1834–2-november-1838/151.

53. "How Firm a Foundation," *Hymns* (Salt Lake City: The Church of Jesus Christ of Latter-day Saints, 1985), no. 85.

54. Francis S. Collins, *The Language of God: A Scientist Presents Evidence for Belief* (New York: Free Press, 2006), 30.

55. Michael Polanyi, *Personal Knowledge* (New York: Harper and Row, 1964).

56. Polanyi, *Personal Knowledge*, 53.

57. Polanyi, *Personal Knowledge*, 53.

58. See Polanyi, *Personal Knowledge*, 62.

59. *Oxford English Dictionary*, online edition.

60. William James, *Essays on Faith and Morals*, ed. Ralph Barton Perry (Cleveland, OH: The World Publishing Company, 1962), 53–54.

61. James, *Essays*, 30–31.

62. James, *Essays*, 24.

63. James, *Essays*, 28.

64. James, *Essays*, 28.

65. Viktor E. Frankl, *Man's Search for Meaning* (Fabler.in/yahoo pdf. Edition, 1959) 4, 37 (quoting Friedrich Nietzsche).

66. Frankl, *Man's Search*, 37.

67. Frankl, *Man's Search*, 33.

68. Viktor Frankl, goodreads.com/quotes/665287-the-meaning-of-life-is-to-give-life -meaning.

69. Frankl, *Man's Search*, 48.

70. George Eliot, "God Needs Antonio," http://www.online-literature.com/george _eliot/3660/.

71. James, *Essays*, 28.

72. Bushman, *Rough Stone Rolling*, 38.

73. Bushman, *Rough Stone Rolling*, 39.

74. Bushman, *Rough Stone Rolling*, 41.

75. Joseph Smith—History 1:33.

76. Bushman, *Rough Stone Rolling*, 44.

77. Bushman, *Rough Stone Rolling*, 40.

78. Bushman, *Rough Stone Rolling*, 118.

79. Bushman, *Rough Stone Rolling*, 187.

80. Bushman, *Rough Stone Rolling*, 193.

Notes

81. http://www.josephsmithpapers.org/paper-summary/history-1838–1856-volume-c-1–2-november-1838-31-july-1842/84.

82. Letter to authors, October 3, 2017; emphasis added.

83. Personal conversation with authors.

84. Thomas H. Greer, *A Brief History of the Western World*, 5th ed. (New York: Harcourt Brace Jovanovich, 1987), 554.

85. Frankl, *Man's Search*, 48.

86. Charles McCurdy, *Modern Art: A Pictorial Anthology* (New York: Macmillan, 1958), 28.

87. N. Berlin, "Traffic of our stage: Why Waiting for Godot?" in *The Massachusetts Review*, Autumn 1999.

88. Berlin, "Traffic."

89. Merriam-Webster online dictionary, "nihilism."

90. *Teachings: Joseph Smith*, 210.

91. See Hal Boyd, "Mormonism's Resolution to One of the Reformation's Most Vexing Riddles," *Deseret News*, November 5, 2017.

92. Khumbulani D. Mdletshe, "A Reflection from an African Convert on Official Declaration 2," *BYU Studies* 55:4 (2016).

93. "Race and the Priesthood," Gospel Topics Essays, lds.org.

94. Peter Wehner, "How Can I Possibly Believe That Faith Is Better Than Doubt?" *New York Times* op-ed, December 25, 2017.

95. "New Mormon leader Russell Nelson pledges to serve God," *Salt Lake Tribune*, January 16, 2018.

96. "Race and the Priesthood," Gospel Topics Essays, lds.org.

97. Dallin H. Oaks, *Life's Lessons Learned* (Salt Lake City: Deseret Book, 2011), 69.

98. Dallin H. Oaks, remarks at "Be One" Celebration, June 1, 2018 (LDS Newsroom).

99. Jana Reiss, "Commentary: Most Mormons still believe the racist priesthood/temple ban was God's will, survey shows," *Salt Lake Tribune*, June 12, 2018.

100. Austen Farrer, quoted in Neal A. Maxwell, "Discipleship and Scholarship," *BYU Studies*, Summer 1992, 5–9.

101. Email from Eric d'Evegnee to Bruce Hafen, February 14, 2018.

102. Email from Kevin Knight to Bruce Hafen, February 14, 2018.

103. Email from Kevin Knight to Bruce Hafen, February 23, 2018.

104. See Spencer W. Kimball, "Peter, My Brother," BYU Devotional, July 13, 1971.

105. Email from Nathan Leonhardt to Bruce Hafen, February 12, 2018.

106. See Hafen and Hafen, *Contrite Spirit*, 124.

107. Fluhman, Flake, and Woodworth, eds., *To Be Learned Is Good*, 295–306.

108. Leo Tolstoy, *War and Peace*, Norton Critical Edition, Maude Trans. (New York: W. W. Norton & Co., 1966), 898–902; emphasis added.

109. Tolstoy, *War and Peace*, 920.

110. Tolstoy, *War and Peace*, 1382, commentary by Nikolai Strakhov.

111. Gordon B. Hinckley, "The Symbol of Our Faith," *Ensign*, May 2005.

112. Hinckley, "Symbol of Our Faith."

113. Neal A. Maxwell, *A Time to Choose* (Salt Lake City: Deseret Book, 1972), 46.

114. "Special Witnesses of Christ: President Faust," https://www.youtube.com/watch?v=VgxandXWbUk.

About the Authors

Bruce C. Hafen was called to the First Quorum of the Seventy in 1996 and has been a General Authority Emeritus since 2010. An internationally recognized family law scholar, he has served as president of BYU–Idaho, dean of the BYU Law School, and provost at BYU. Two of his past books won the year's best book award from Deseret Book: *The Broken Heart* in 1989 and *A Disciple's Life: The Biography of Neal A. Maxwell* in 2002. He recently served as president of the St. George Utah Temple.

Marie K. Hafen has taught at BYU–Idaho, the University of Utah, and BYU–Provo—classes in Shakespeare, writing, and Book of Mormon. She has been a contributing author to several books, including, with her husband, *Covenant Hearts: Why Marriage Matters and How to Make it Last* (2005) and *The Contrite Spirit: How the Temple Helps Us Apply Christ's Atonement* (2015). She has served on the Young Women General Board, on the *Deseret News* board of directors, and as matron of the St. George Utah Temple.

The Hafens are most grateful to be the parents of seven children and grandparents of forty-six.